Praise for Antony Sher's Falstaff

'A lust for wine, women and mischief are the hallmarks of Falstaff, one of Shakespeare's greatest characters. All these outsize appetites shine through Antony Sher's marvellous performance... But more than anything, it is Falstaff's relish for language – his unstemmed and unstemmable gift for elaborate prevarication, for colourful excoriation, for creative ingratiation – that Mr Sher brings to buoyant life.' *New York Times*

'Antony Sher as the roguish fat knight and "corrupter of youth", Falstaff, is tremendous.' *The Times*

'He has played Richard III, Shylock, Leontes, Macbeth and Prospero to huge acclaim. But can Sir Antony Sher, one of our most Shakespeare-steeped theatrical knights, give us a Falstaff to remember? ... The answer is yes.' *Daily Telegraph*

'Antony Sher's magnificent and exquisitely pitched Falstaff is at the heart of this beautifully detailed production.' *Financial Times*

'Like Robert Stephens in 1991, Sher reminds us that Falstaff is one of nature's predators. Sher plays down the fatness to emphasise the knight's upper-class origins. But, just as you start to warm to this Falstaff, you are reminded of his rapacity... A magnificent, magnetic performance.' *Guardian*

'It is Sher's irrepressible Falstaff that will linger in the memory – a lord of misrule who's absurd, delightful and in the end deeply sad.' *Evening Standard*

'Everything about his performance is superb – the delivery, the warmth, Falstaff's arrogance and his manipulation of those around him, and that great speech on the eve of war on the perversity of honour is moving and powerful.' *Huffington Post*

Also by Antony Sher

Fiction

Cheap Lives
The Feast
Indoor Boy
Middlepost

Non-Fiction

Beside Myself
Primo Time
Woza Shakespeare!
(*co-written with Gregory Doran*)
Year of the King

Stage Plays

The Giant
I.D.

TV Filmscript

Changing Step

Paintings and Drawings

Characters

Antony Sher

YEAR OF
THE FAT KNIGHT

The Falstaff Diaries

with illustrations by the author

NICK HERN BOOKS
London
www.nickhernbooks.co.uk

A Nick Hern Book

Year of the Fat Knight first published in Great Britain in 2015 by
Nick Hern Books Limited, The Glasshouse, 49a Goldhawk Road,
London W12 8QP

Cover photo by Kwame Lestrade
Author photo by Paul Stuart
Designed and typeset by Nick Hern Books, London

Printed and bound in Great Britain by CPI Group (UK) Ltd

A CIP catalogue record for this book is available
from the British Library

ISBN 978 1 84842 461 6

For Verne

Contents

Year of the Fat Knight

1. A Fat Knight?

Monday 11 February 2013

It's all Ian McKellen's fault.

A month or so ago, Greg (Doran; Royal Shakespeare Company Artistic Director, and my partner) was talking to Ian about whether he'd like to come back to the company, and what parts he might play. Greg mentioned that he was directing *Henry IV Parts I* and *II* next year, and what about Falstaff? Ian said it wasn't of interest to him, and then added, 'But why are you looking for Falstaff when you're living with him?' Ian was making reference to a performance of mine that he'd seen at the National Theatre: Jacob in *Travelling Light*. Nicky Wright's play is about the early days of film-making, set in an East European shtetl, circa 1900, and Jacob is the local timber merchant (and embryonic movie mogul), described in the stage directions as 'a big and ebullient man, a Tolstoyan peasant'. As a character, he is what is called larger-than-life. And yes, looking back now, I suppose Jacob could have been Falstaff's Jewish cousin.

Anyway, Greg told me what Ian had said, and we smiled at it, and didn't take it seriously at all. Falstaff has never been a part I've remotely thought of as being mine.

Casting it has preoccupied Greg for a couple of years now, and I've been his sounding board from time to time. All sorts of names have been mooted – including Patrick Stewart, Jim Broadbent, Brian Cox – but Greg eventually decided his first choice was Derek Jacobi. The offer is presently with him.

Self as Jacob

Today we drove from our home in Islington up to Oxford University, where Greg will be this year's Humanitas Visiting Professor of Drama. The first event takes place this evening, an *In Conversation* with him and me, chaired by Shakespeare scholar Jonathan Bate.

In the car, Greg mentioned that he suspected Derek was going to say no to Falstaff, because of other commitments. Greg said he'd found himself really taking stock. I thought he'd changed the subject when now he suddenly started talking about my two performances at the NT – Jacob in *Travelling Light* and Voigt in *The Captain of Köpenick* (which opened last week):

'Both times you've surprised me, and it's nice that can still happen – I would have thought I knew your full range. But there was something about the size and earthiness of Jacob, the mischief of Voigt... well, they were things I hadn't really seen before. I think Ian might be right. I think you could play Falstaff. Why don't you read it?'

I stared out of the car window at the countryside around the M40, familiar from a thousand drives to and from Stratford – there had been snow during the night and it was still falling lightly. I didn't know how to react to Greg. I had no problem about not being the first choice for the part – if you live with a director, you understand the nature of these things – but the idea was still baffling. Me as Falstaff? Short, Jewish, gay, South African me as Shakespeare's gigantically big, rudely hetero, quintessentially English, Fat Knight? It made no sense.

But this is an ongoing problem for the character actor. He never feels ideally right for any part.

I said, 'Well… let's talk about it again… if Derek says no.' And we moved on to other things.

In Oxford, we were given an attic room overlooking the quad in one of the colleges, Brasenose. At 5 p.m. we did our event, which was really quite easy: talking about three of our Shakespeare collaborations – *Titus Andronicus*, *Winter's Tale* and *Macbeth* – illustrated with clips from the filmed versions. Then drinks in the college with the principal, and dinner at High Table. It's another world…

Tuesday 12 February

Greg stayed in Oxford (he's doing a series of talks and masterclasses over the next few days) while I returned to London.

Köpenick has been out of the NT repertoire for a few days, so we had a line-run this afternoon. Must say I went into the room with a heavy heart. We had some mixed reviews last week, and a real stinker on Sunday. (I don't read reviews, but I get told the score – the star ratings – and the *Sunday Times* gave us only two.) I felt vaguely embarrassed in front of the company; as the leading actor, I was involved in the whole gestation of the show. But I needn't have worried. Actors are a buoyant breed. I don't know if any individuals were disappointed by the reviews, but as a group they were full of energy and laughter today, and full-throated in the big sing-songs, and passionate about keeping the fights and dances in tip-top shape. The session really lifted my spirits.

And the show itself was good this evening, with a big, warm audience.

So far, touch wood, no real damage from any of the negative reviews.

But the experience has unsettled me. I saw the 1972 NT production of *Köpenick*, with Paul Scofield as Voigt, and Frank Dunlop directing John Mortimer's very witty adaptation of Zuckmayer's original. It was a fine piece of theatre, and much acclaimed. Currently we've got a spectacular production by Adrian Noble, and a gritty new version by Ron Hutchinson, but the critics just haven't come to the party. It has shaken my faith in my own judgement.

So the Falstaff idea isn't coming at a great time...

Wednesday 13 February

Greg rang from Oxford. He's just spoken to Derek Jacobi, who has said no. Not because of other commitments, but because he's reread it and can't see himself in the role.

'So,' said Greg; 'I am now officially proposing that *you* do it.'

After a pause, I said, 'I'll think about it, okay?' Then put the phone down, feeling I'd just had bad news.

Friday 15 February

Greg was appointed to the post of Artistic Director – we call it The Job – in April 2012, but he's only been fully in charge since September. As he finds his legs, he's being helped by a formidably good PA, Jane Tassell. She sees it as one of her many duties to ensure that he has proper holidays, and since holidays have always been an important part of our relationship, Jane constantly checks Greg's work schedule against mine, and marks out possible breaks. She then fiercely monitors Greg's diary, keeping these periods clear. He's been very busy recently, and I've been opening *Köpenick*. So, with another substantial gap in my NT performances coming up, we're grabbing a holiday in Kenya. It's next week, so there's not much time to properly consider Falstaff. Despite a career of doing classical theatre, I still find Shakespeare difficult to read. Over the last two days, I've been inching through Falstaff's scenes – just them, not the whole plays – with the aid of the RSC's excellent new edition (co-edited by Jonathan Bate and Eric Rasmussen), using both the notes at the bottom of each page and the synopsis of scenes at the end.

Some first impressions that surprised me:

- On three occasions in *Part I*, Falstaff resolves to clean up his act ('I must give over this life', 'I'll repent suddenly', 'I'll leave sack'), and yet in *Part II* his biggest, most celebratory speech is a hymn to alcohol ('If I had a thousand sons, the first principle I would teach them should be to addict themselves to sack!'). I sense the circular rhythms of serious dependency here. Rather than just a jolly old bloke who likes his drink. Could one play him with serious dependency?
- His imagination. Whether talking about Bardolph's nose or Shallow's nakedness there's a hugely inventive, colourful mind at work.
- His heartlessness. Not just the famous speech about soldiers being 'food for powder' (cannon fodder), but he's a dangerous friend – he'll rubbish you behind your back without a thought. He does this to Shallow, to Hal, to Poins, and others.
- His charm. People like Mistress Quickly know he's a shit, yet love him.

As well as reading the text, I have a recent performance in mind. Normally, I'd avoid seeing another actor play a part I was considering, but it's too late this time. I watched the BBC TV series *The Hollow Crown* last year, with Simon Russell Beale playing Falstaff in the *Henries*. But I don't feel intimidated – it was too individualistic an interpretation. Not so much a life force as a death's head, intensely haunted by his own mortality. Really came into his own in *Part II*, as did Richard Eyre's film – a great melancholic picture of England as a sick land. This was so good, that for the first time I wondered if *Part II* wasn't the better play.

Reporting back to Greg, I say, 'Falstaff is not a great part.'

'What?!'

'It's two great parts.'

'Ah. Right. Is that a yes then?'

'No. I can't easily see myself as him. I keep thinking – why me? Just because I've put on a bit of weight and I've got the title, why should I be the Fat Knight?'

We laugh, but my doubts are serious, and real.

Sunday 17 February

It's crazy. Today's *Observer* published a list of top power couples. Which included Bill and Hillary Clinton, Chairman and Madame Mao, Beyoncé and Jay Z, and *us*.

Simon Russell Beale as Falstaff

'How on earth did we get on that?' I asked.

'They must've wanted to tick the gay box,' Greg replied.

Over lunch at the Almeida Restaurant, we discussed the Falstaff situation. Greg asked me to explain my reservations.

'Well, there's "the look", of course,' I said.

'Every Falstaff has to wear a fat suit.'

'Yes, yes, and anyway it's my thing. Richard III didn't just have a prosthetic hump, but big muscular arms and twisted knees too, the young Tamburlaine had to be athletic, the old one was obese, there was Cyrano and his nose, there was…'

'You can change yourself… you're a "shape-shifter".'

'But it's not just Falstaff's shape. There's something about his spirit. That's the truly big bit of him.'

'You could do it.'

'Then why haven't I been thought of before? You've talked about all sorts of actors. We've talked about them together. I've never been in the frame. Never – in either of our heads.'

'And that's fine,' said Greg confidently. 'Happens all the time in casting. The best idea, the person you end up with, wasn't even on your original list.'

'Well… there's something else. And it's not easy to talk about.'

Greg frowned. This wasn't like us.

I proceeded slowly: 'We're in a funny position. That crazy *Observer* thing about power couples. I mean, when we met, I was already established, you were starting out… and yet now, in terms of power, you're much more powerful than me. You know I have no problem with that. You know I rejoice in you having The Job. But with something like this, where I'm a completely left-field idea for the part, and maybe completely wrong… we could be accused of nepotism.'

'Oh that's nonsense – you're a leading classical actor!'

'You're not thinking about this properly. Nepotism. I mean it seriously. I'd hate that charge to be made. I'd hate it for you especially. And actually it could be bad for you – this early on in The Job – if you get this wrong.'

'I'm not getting this wrong.'

Greg was calm. I was not.

He said, 'And if it's of any comfort to you, the Board would have to ratify your casting. It comes under a clause called Conflict of

Interests. At the next Board meeting, I'd have to step out of the room while they discussed exactly what you're scared of – the question of nepotism.' He paused. 'So how do we proceed?'

'I need advice from someone who's outside us… but someone who knows the business. Paul is coming to see *Köpenick* when we get back from Kenya…' (Paul Lyon-Maris, my agent) '…We're having dinner. He'll be good to talk to. He'll tell me straight.'

'Right.'

'And now I think we need to change the subject. Don't you?'

'I do.' Leaning forward, his face alight, he gave a whispered shout: 'We're going on holiday!'

Wednesday 20 February

Africa.

There's nothing like it to clear the mind and refresh the soul. We regularly visit South Africa, my homeland, to see my family, but occasionally we go to East Africa for the real thing. Wild Africa.

We're in the Maasai Mara on the Serengeti, staying in a tent camp called Cottar's, which is designed in a colonial 1920s style, the period of big-game hunting – then done with rifles, now with cameras.

Our jeep is open (canvas roof but no sides), thank goodness – you don't always get these in East Africa – and our guide/ranger is a warm, wise man who asks us to call him G-G. He has a young Maasai tracker with him.

Over the years, we've done so many game drives in so many different reserves, that it's easy to become complacent. But this morning, we had a truly exciting time, with viewings of three of the big five: we rode alongside a pride of lions on the move, complete with big males and cubs of different ages, some very small and cute; a family of elephants, with young too; and a massive herd of buffalo. Also saw giraffe, a huge eland bull, and a cheetah atop a termite hill.

But it isn't only the animals. More often it's the place itself. On the dusk drive yesterday, one half of the landscape lay under a biblical spectacle of sun shafts and cloud shadows, while the other had a tranquil, delicate, almost underwater light. It was the most magical vision. I held my breath. Which happened again this afternoon, when we went to the open savannahs, the oceans of yellow-green grass. We stopped for sundowners (the jeeps carry iceboxes with drinks of your choice) on a little rocky island with one tree, an umbrella thorn acacia, and from that standpoint, you could turn three hundred and sixty degrees and see nothing but the rolling plains and the huge, climbing sky. This was the Africa of fantasy, of dreams, of legend. It was like civilisation had never happened.

Laurens van der Post describes it beautifully in this piece, which Greg found in a book of essays: 'What wilderness does is present us with a blueprint, as it were, of what creation was about in the beginning, when all the plants and trees and animals were magnetic, fresh from the hands of whatever created them. This blueprint is still there, and those of us who see it find an incredible nostalgia rising in us, an impulse to return and discover it again.'

Tuesday 26 February

We're spending the second half of our trip on the coast just below Mombasa, in a hotel called the Alfajiri Villas.

This is the part where we holiday properly, doing nothing at all. Other than swim, sunbathe, read, eat and drink. We have a pool on the patio of our villa, but we prefer the sea. The best local beach is Congo (where the Congo River flows in), about 3km north, a forty-five-minute walk along the sands. We have to be accompanied by a member of the hotel staff. This is not to protect us from Somali pirates (though we've heard some grisly stories), but from what are called the beach boys. These are hawkers who pester tourists with their goods. And will snatch cameras and bags too. They're pretty relentless. You feel like a wildebeest trying to take a stroll through a pack of hyenas. So we're grateful for our bodyguard. The other, unaccompanied white visitors on the shoreline, who all seem to be elderly Germans, their skin sunburned to a wrinkled, leathery finish, look rather vulnerable. Anyway, it's worth it when we get to the other end. The beach is on a slope below some magnificently gross baobabs – the Falstaff of trees! – and the water of the Indian Ocean, on the Equator, is blissful.

Talking of Falstaff, we're having pre-dinner drinks on our patio this evening, when Greg suddenly says, lightly, tentatively, 'We haven't really mentioned the *Henries*.'

'No. But I've been thinking about it.'

'And – ?'

'I just have this image... an awful image... of people laughing at me. For thinking I could play him. For having the chutzpah.'

Greg smiles. 'You've never been short of chutzpah.'

'It's the Shakespeare biggies, isn't it? They're in a different league, on a different scale. You can't get it wrong. Well, I mean you can get the playing of them wrong – there are a hundred wrong things you can do in rehearsals, or in the design, or whatever – but what you can't get wrong is the starting point. Your own certainty that you're right for the part.'

'Were you absolutely certain you were right for Macbeth... Leontes... Prospero...?'

'No, I wasn't, you know I wasn't, yet they still felt within reach. But there's something about Falstaff. He's just so... iconic.'

Greg sighs. Tries to talk about the other casting. The title role, King Henry IV, is one of the hardest parts to cast in Shakespeare. It needs a leading actor, but leading actors don't want to play it. Henry is written as a very angry man, and there's a deadly temptation to just shout your way through every scene.

Greg and I agree that the best Henry we've seen was Jeremy Irons in the *Hollow Crown* series. He was a brooding, haunted man, endlessly fascinating. The part suddenly seemed like a great part. We bumped into Jeremy at a Christmas party a couple of months ago, and complimented him on his performance. He said he could never have done it in the theatre. The camera allowed options – degrees of introspection – that just wouldn't be available on stage.

Tonight Greg says, 'Obviously I can't cast Henry till I've cast Falstaff, but I've got some good ideas. Can I tell you?'

I feel uncomfortable. In the circumstances, I don't want to play this casting game.

Suddenly, the waiter Ifrahiem is at our side. 'The monkeys!' he announces with a grin.

We've been enchanted by a family of colobus monkeys who come into the trees around our villa at about this time each day. Greg has been trying to photograph them – their black faces peering at us through the leaves – and runs for the camera.

I'm relieved. Saved by the monkeys!

Monday 4 March

Back in London.

I'm impressed by the NT. They seem to have scheduled *Köpenick* perfectly – giving it just a limited number of performances – and combined with the fact that they have a big, loyal, mailing-list audience, this has meant that we've played to full, warm houses (which is not always the case in the Olivier). This has allowed my performance to thrive. I'm very fond of my character, Wilhelm Voigt, a street rat, a Chaplinesque tramp, a little *nebbish*, who gets his five minutes of fame when he impersonates an army captain. It's hard to believe now that I had as much doubt about my suitability for this role as I currently feel about Falstaff. I had a real crisis before rehearsals began, convincing myself that I was wrong for the part – it needed a cheeky Cockney chappie, a young Bob Hoskins – and that I'd be crucified. In retrospect, it was probably a subconscious insecurity about the play itself, for indeed it was the play and not my performance that has been criticised. [*Photo insert, page 1, Self as Voigt*]

My agent, Paul Lyon-Maris, had to miss the opening, and came along tonight. We dined in the NT restaurant, the Mezzanine, afterwards. Paul is a neat, fit chap with a dark little smile, in his early fifties, a horse-rider in his spare time, and one of the most powerful agents in the business. He'd liked the show, liked me, and especially praised Adrian Noble's production.

We got down to business. Last year, I played Freud in a successful revival of Terry Johnson's play *Hysteria* – directed by the author – at the Theatre Royal in Bath, and ever since then there have been efforts to give it a future life. A West End transfer was mooted, but hasn't materialised. More excitingly, there have been plans to take it to Broadway, where Terry is better known as a director (*La Cage aux Folles* and the Judy Garland play, *End of the Rainbow*) than as a writer. It's thought that New Yorkers would particularly relish this play, being about Freud and Dalí. These two legends are the stars of the show, but the main role is actually a young woman, Jessica, and the American producers have been trying to find a big name, a film actress, to play it. Tonight Paul said it was still on the cards, and that if it happened it would be in the autumn. Which would clash with the *Henry IV*s – they start rehearsals in December.

We discussed Falstaff. I asked two questions: was the idea of me playing him ludicrous, and could Greg and I be accused of nepotism? Paul answered no, emphatically, to both. Which was good to hear – he doesn't bullshit. On the other hand, he didn't say, you *must* play Falstaff. But then, that isn't his style either. As a good agent he knows that his clients have to make important decisions by themselves. He can advise, he can't dictate. And in this case, he probably also feels a special challenge: tiptoeing around my relationship with Greg. It must seem like a bit of a minefield.

He suggested that the RSC should make an official offer of Falstaff, through him. He could then use it to sharpen the concentration of the American producers of *Hysteria*. If it came to a choice between the two, we'd face that at a later date.

As I travelled home, I thought that if it did come to a choice, Freud would certainly be the safer option. I've never had any doubts about my ability to play him, except that, ironically, I'm not *thin* enough: the play is set in 1938, when he was dying of mouth cancer, couldn't eat properly, and looked skeletal.

Friday 8 March

With my decision on hold, in limbo, Greg suggested I do some reading about the role: 'Have a look at Harold Bloom's book, he's got a whole chapter on Falstaff.'

Harold Bloom, the Big Daddy of American Shakespeare Scholarship, and author of the tome, *Shakespeare: The Invention of the Human*.

Diving into Bloom's book, I find that he rates Falstaff very highly indeed – alongside Hamlet, as Shakespeare's greatest creations.

That comes as a surprise. It sends a prickle of excitement, and danger, up my spine.

I jot some notes:

- Falstaff is neither immoral or amoral, but of another realm.
- He is 'one of the lords of language'… 'the monarch of language'… his is 'a festival of language'.
- How did Hal and Falstaff enter into their original friendship? Why choose Falstaff as your mentor?
- Falstaff is an old warrior. A veteran soldier, turned drunk and highwayman. This makes a lot of sense to me. When Hal gives him

a regiment to command, Falstaff's behaviour is totally in keeping with someone who knows the reality of war and is thoroughly cynical about it: your soldiers *are* just cannon fodder.

These are dark things. I like them. It's more like the kind of stuff I play. I suppose it's the usual problem of doing Shakespeare's great roles: you have to see past what I call the Stratford-souvenir-shop image – in this case, a merry old buffer with tankard of ale – and look at what Shakespeare actually wrote.

Sunday 10 March

We went to a flat-warming party for Simon Callow and his new partner, Sebastian Fox, who is in his thirties, beautiful, charming, half-German, a management consultant. They've been together for about a year, and have now taken this major step of setting up home together. It was very touching, and we were delighted to raise a glass to them.

A refreshing aspect of the party was that many of the guests were Sebastian's friends, who knew nothing about theatre. When they asked what we did, I replied, 'I'm an actor, and Greg runs the Royal Shakespeare Company.' I still feel an enormous amount of pleasure saying that aloud. There's a Jewish word *nachas*, meaning the joy that a parent feels in the achievements of their children. With Greg only ten years my junior, it doesn't really apply to us, but I'm nevertheless getting an awful lot of *nachas*...!

So, Simon and I both have younger partners now. Not that we're in competition any more. Actually, it was only ever from my point of view. As a young actor, I regarded him as my arch-rival, and couldn't be in the same room as him. These days, we're the best of friends, and I think of him as someone who is especially knowledgeable about our business.

Today, I was very tempted to take him aside, and say, 'Listen, I've been asked to play Falstaff – just tell me the truth, is it a good idea?'

(I need *someone*, other than Greg, to say it's a good idea.)

Trouble is, Simon has played Falstaff twice: in Greg's production of *Merry Wives: The Musical* at Stratford, and in Orson Welles's *Chimes at Midnight* (the stage version which Welles later filmed) at Chichester. I suspect he might regard it as his part, and might not be able to give the most objective advice.

So I didn't mention it.

Simon Callow as Falstaff (in "Merry Wives, The Musical")

Monday 11 March

The weather has become intensely cold, and little flakes of snow are falling.

I feel a serious onset of the Monday-morning blues, what with Greg leaving for work and me stuck in the house for the day. I find refuge in Simon Callow's thoughts on Falstaff. I may not have heard them from the horse's mouth yesterday, but I can still read about them. Writing for the Faber series, *Actors on Shakespeare*, Simon did two small paperbacks (for *Parts I* and *II*) on Falstaff.

Talking frankly of his experience of the *Chimes at Midnight* play, which compresses Shakespeare's double into one, focusing mainly on Falstaff, Simon says that it 'lumbers across the stage unhappily and unrhythmically, dangerously risking overexposure for the Fat Knight.' That's interesting. Falstaff may be a fabulous creation, but if he was a foodstuff he'd be an excessively rich pudding, and you can't have a whole meal of that. In the full version of the *Henries*,

Shakespeare serves out the portions judiciously, intercut with other stories.

Like Harold Bloom, Simon has some vivid descriptions of Falstaff:

- 'mighty pagan creature'
- 'his sense of self is so overpowering that he sees himself as the source of all things'
- 'a great escapologist... a Houdini of the mind'
- 'the world always seems a larger place when Falstaff speaks.'

There's a lot about the sheer *size* of the man, which makes me self-conscious again. The actor really needs to be tall as well as fat; Hal calls him 'a huge hill of flesh'. Yet it's ridiculous – I'm about the same height as the two Simons – Callow and Russell Beale – yet somehow they're regarded as ideal and natural Falstaffs, and I'm not. I'm still scrabbling around for a foothold on this hill of flesh...!

Tuesday 12 March

'Hugh Griffith wasn't a tall man.'

This was John Barton's response when Greg asked him this afternoon. Greg goes to visit John regularly in his London flat, and I think of the two of them as the Spirits of RSC Past and RSC Present, in wise consultation with one another.

Hugh Griffith played Falstaff in the famous production of the *Henries* which John co-directed with Peter Hall at Stratford in 1964. I'm intrigued by the thought of Griffith in the part, because as a film actor he made a strong impression on me in my youth, as the Arab Sheikh who teaches Charlton Heston to ride chariots in *Ben Hur*, and the Squire in *Tom Jones*. There was, in those big eyes and even bigger eyebrows, a wicked glint. I didn't know he was also a stage actor. What was he like as Falstaff? John told Greg he couldn't really remember, apart from him getting drunker and drunker during the alcohol speech, and some business with a real donkey. (When was that, for heaven's sake – one of the Gloucestershire scenes?) But maybe John was just being diplomatic, because when they revived the *Henries* in 1966, Griffith had left, and Falstaff was then played by Paul Rogers.

It turns out I can judge for myself. An audio recording of Griffith as Falstaff exists. A few years ago, working with the British Library Sound Archive, Greg produced two double CDs for the RSC, called

The Essential Shakespeare, featuring scenes from some of their most famous productions, with their most famous actors, including Paul Robeson as Othello and Olivier as Coriolanus. Recorded in performance, with the noise of the audience – laughter and coughs – and the clump of actors' feet on the stage-boards, the atmosphere is so unmistakably *live* you gain a clear glimpse of this long-lost work. It's so much better than a studio recording, and somehow even more vivid than photographs.

And so I listen to Hugh Griffith and Ian Holm (Hal) doing the 'play within the play' in the tavern scene (Act Two, Scene Four in *Part I*), when Falstaff and Hal take turns to be King Henry in the act of remonstrating his wayward son. Griffith uses his own Welsh accent as Falstaff, which works well, giving him a rough-and-ready manner, both jokey and combative.

So here is a very distinctive Falstaff, short and Welsh, tailored to this particular actor's style, and succeeding splendidly.

He was a personality actor – he makes the part come to him.

I am a character actor – I go to the part.

Can I go to this one?

Wednesday 13 March

'Piss or get off the pot.'

Greg says this lightly, but I've heard it before – when actors keep him waiting to say yes or no to an offer – and I know he's running out of patience. My inability to make a decision means that we're both stuck to the spot. He can't move on: find another Falstaff, or cast the other parts. If it was another director, I wouldn't care about their problems – this is too important a decision for me – but it isn't another director, it's Greg.

He's driving to Stratford this morning. I've got three *Köpenick*s, and then I'll go up by train on Friday. At the last moment, I put my drawing board and paper into the car for him to take along. I've an image in my mind, which I need to sketch out during next week, something which might help the situation...

Hugh Griffith as Felstaff

Sunday 17 March

Stratford.

'Greater love hath no man than this,' I said grimly as we left our Avonside flat, 'than to give up a Sunday evening to see a school play!'

But it was a special occasion. And Greg wanted to attend.

One hundred years ago, in 1913, KES (King Edward VI School in Stratford, where Shakespeare was a pupil) did *Henry V* as their annual play. A few years later, almost half of the school's pupils (thirty out of sixty-nine) were dead, killed in the First World War.

Tonight's performance – of *Henry V* – was to commemorate them. We had drinks at the school, in Shakespeare's classroom, with speeches and a poignant display of photos from the 1913 production – schoolboys in stage armour – then walked down Chapel Lane to the Swan for the show.

The cast did well, aided by a professional actor as the Chorus: Tim Pigott-Smith, an ex-student (and head boy) of KES. But I'm afraid I always struggle with *Henry V* as a play. Hal has lost all the complexity which makes him so fascinating in the *Henries*, and is now just a rather heroic chap going to war. And apart from the Chorus, there's no one else that really grabs my attention.

But, but, but... there is Shakespeare. I was sitting back in a slight daze, when suddenly a minor character, the soldier Williams, did a speech which brought me to the edge of my seat:

> The king himself hath a heavy reckoning to make, when all those legs and arms and heads, chopped off in a battle, shall join together at the latter day, and cry all, 'We died at such a place' – some swearing, some crying for a surgeon, some upon their wives left poor behind them... I am afeard there are few die well that die in a battle, for how can they charitably dispose of anything, when blood is their argument?

Jesus. Not only is it an eloquent and horrific image of war, but it's like a piece of surrealism, picturing the gathering of dismembered limbs.

Simon Callow says something similar in his book on *Henry IV Part I*. Writing about Falstaff's bizarre behaviour on the battlefield, picking over Sir Walter Blunt's corpse, and offering Hal a bottle of sack from his pistol holster, Simon describes it as a scene that could have been written by Ionesco: 'At moments like these, Shakespeare seems to have within him the whole of the subsequent development of Western drama.'

After the show, we said a quick hello to Tim Pigott-Smith. As we walked home, Greg said, 'He'd be a fine Henry IV.'

'Mm-mh,' I replied, again refusing to play the casting game.

Monday 18 March

Beautiful sunshine. The Avon ablaze with light. And very high: a fast-flowing, coffee-coloured swell, spilling over the opposite bank.

The French windows of our ground-floor flat are just three metres from the river, but the slope of the land is such that we never get flooded – it always goes over the other side.

We're in a red-brick block which the RSC built as company digs, after knocking down the original Avonside, a gloriously run-down old mansion, where I had some rooms during my first season in 1982, and which my dad described as 'the ghost house' when my parents visited that year.

The flat itself is fairly basic, but the view from our front room is a source of constant inspiration. The river is mesmerising in any weather situation. Greg and I fight over this room, both wanting it as our study – the alternative is the back bedroom (which has a decent view of Trinity Church) – but it's mostly not a problem: when we're in Stratford together, he's usually working in his office at the RSC headquarters on Chapel Lane, and the beautiful room is mine.

As it is today, when I set up my easel, my drawing board, and a sheet of the thick, textured paper on which I like to sketch these days: it's meant for watercolours, but I use Caran d'Ache crayons. It's a self-portrait I want to do.

I know the title. 'A Fat Knight?' Specifically 'a' rather than 'the', and the question mark is also key. This is not to be an image of Falstaff, but of myself thinking about playing Falstaff. I want to try and capture the difficulty of the decision.

In 1996 I was in a clinic for cocaine dependency, and one of the things that helped my recovery (which I'm happy to report is intact to this day) was art therapy. It's like psychotherapy, except you create an image first, and then any words come second: how it makes you feel, how it depicts current anxieties. Today's exercise is similar.

I sit alongside a big, free-standing mirror, half turned towards it. The extra pounds which I've gained recently are at their broadest and ugliest at this angle. I emphasise the bulge of my stomach, almost as if wearing a fat suit. I want my face clear of my specs, so I hold them in my left hand, while my right reaches forward with the crayon.

So here I sit: me in this room, and me in the mirror, and me on the paper. All of us in quiet contemplation of one another.

As the drawing develops, I'm intrigued by the expression on the face. A slight frown – in fact, my short-sightedness – reading as a slight scowl.

Something dull and sour. Boredom. There have been times here, some Avonside afternoons, when I've been out of work as an actor, and I have no writing project on the go, and I am suffering from painter's block. Then I can feel a kind of self-disgust – the workaholic without his drug of choice, no hit, no quick fix, just time passing very slowly.

Isn't that reason enough to do Falstaff – a work project so big I'll not be bored for years?

No. It isn't enough.

Then what about the simple fact that it's another great Shakespeare role? I'm proud of the Shakespeare notches on my belt, and here would be one more, a giant one, a fabulous one, and one I never dreamed of. How could I *not* do it?

Well, why didn't McKellen or Jacobi do it? They've both spent their careers notching up a line of Shakespeares, and they've done their Lears now, and there's nothing left. What was it about Falstaff that they shied away from? Maybe a generational thing. They're the last group from a theatrical tradition which said that, for the classical actor, certain roles (like Hamlet, Macbeth, etc.) lead to Lear, while others (like Touchstone, Bottom, etc.) lead to Falstaff, and never the twain shall meet.

This is a blind alley. You can't judge yourself against other actors. *What is it then? Why is this decision harder than any other?*

Look at the eyes in the portrait. Half-closed. Defensive.

The thing I've said again and again is that I don't want to be laughed at.

Where is this from – this fear? Me at school, me in the army. Short and weedy – feeble at sport, at marching, at running up fucking sand dunes with a weight on my back.

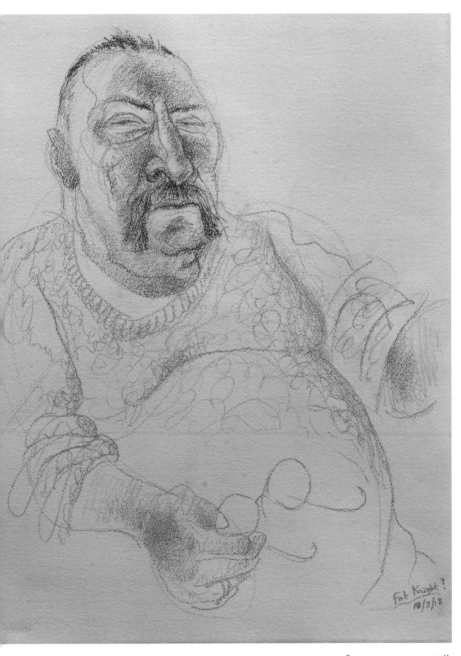

"A Fat Knight ?"

And here we are again – the little guy trying to be a big guy. Scared of failing, scared of mockery.

The portrait is finished. The man in it just looks pissed off now. Paralysed by indecision.

Something is going to have to happen to break this.

When Greg came home, I showed him the picture, thinking he'd disapprove. It's an unflattering image of his chap, after all. But he liked it as a drawing – said it was very economic, very assured, very free. That cheered me up.

Thursday 21 March

Köpenick back in the repertoire. But I've brought a bad cough back from Stratford (maybe the 'river cough' which Greg and I seem to catch sometimes when we stay at Avonside). One of the craziest things actors have to do is perform when ill. In any other job, you'd just go home to bed.

The experience was dreamlike, or rather nightmarish. My entire focus went off my performance and onto my cough. I was engaged in a battle – between the huge amount of text I had to speak and the tiny but deadly tickle in my throat. Would I get through the next line, the next speech? Was it safe to turn my head, to sit or stand? I carried a hipflask of water in my costume, in case of choking emergencies, but, for the most part, stage adrenalin – Doctor Theatre – held these off. Then I'd go back to my dressing room and hack my guts out.

Tonight's audience was quiet, and for the first time the applause didn't lift when I took my solo bow in the curtain call. Nor did it deserve to. I was definitely 'under', as they say.

What a wretched evening.

Friday 22 March

I said something would have to happen, and this morning it does.

All alone in the house, I have an outburst of fury. At my cough, at last night's performance, at *Köpenick* itself. Funny, but now that I'm not well, I'm suddenly aware of the show not being well either. I mean, at its heart, Zuckmayer's play just isn't good enough! And it's happened to me before. *Kean* in the West End. Sartre's play just wasn't good enough! It's not good enough to have a good part if the play isn't good enough!!

And here I am now, with Falstaff – being offered not just a good part, but a great one, in two plays which are not just good, but great. And am I seriously farting and faffing around, wondering whether to do it or not?!

Fuck tradition, fuck the normal notions of who should play Falstaff, fuck its status as an iconic role, fuck the fact that I'm not fat enough or tall enough or whatever...!

I'm a character actor, and this is the greatest character part ever written. It presents me with a tremendous feast of the kind of acting that I like best, that I do best – it'll take all my imagination and creativity to invent his shape, his voice, his very being, and I will enjoy doing that. And yes, it's a humungous job, and will feed my workaholism to the limit, and that *is* important, and I'll enjoy that too. And Greg and I will be working together on Shakespeare again, and I will especially enjoy that.

It seems only polite to tell Paul Lyon-Maris first, in case there's any news on the Broadway production of *Hysteria* – though if it came to a clean choice now between the Thin Professor or the Fat Knight, I'd go with the latter.

I put in a call to Paul, but can't get hold of him straight away.

And then a strange little domestic crisis suddenly propels things along. Our cooker has been ropey for some time. The dial for the oven is loose, and given this is a gas appliance it's dangerous. At lunchtime I'm about to bake some fishcakes when I notice that the oven is warm, even though the dial is turned to 'off' and there's no flame. Greg cooked last night, and somehow it's stayed warm since then. Being the least domesticated person in the world – my excuse is, 'I'm a white South African' – I don't know what to do. Try ringing Greg but his answer machine is on. Leave a message. Then go out and buy fish 'n' chips.

When I return, I find that the loose dial can be turned off further, and then the warmth inside does finally fade.

Greg rings, concerned by the anxiety in my voice on the message. We agree that the cooker is now unusable, and we'll have to get a new one.

As we're finishing the call, I say, 'By the way, I hoped to talk to Paul before you, but he hasn't rung back yet... anyway, I'm going to do Falstaff.'

Greg goes silent, then gives a whoop of joy. 'We are going to have such an adventure!' Then he's silent. Then says, 'I'm crying… I'm in the middle of Tottenham Court Road, and I'm crying.'

After the call, I feel an enormous surge of relief – and excitement.

I scoff my fish 'n' chips, then email Paul with the news. He's still not available, but his second-in-command, Nick Forgacs, rings back immediately. Tells me that he's thrilled – the *Henries* are his favourite plays, and he thinks I've made absolutely the right decision. I've been waiting for *someone* to say it's a good idea. 'Thank you!' I reply.

Back at home after tonight's show, I open a bottle of champagne. Greg asks, 'What was the deciding factor?'

'My cough,' I answer.

'What?'

'No. In the end it's just about… character acting.'

'Mm-mh?'

'Anyway, to our big adventure.' I lift my glass. 'And to…'

We say it together: '…The Fat Knight!'

2. Character Acting

What is character acting?

This question arose as I was clearing a part of my London study today and came across a photo of my giant painting *The Audience*. Done in 2009, it's an autobiographical piece, showing about a hundred and fifty people sitting in a dilapidated theatre auditorium. There are groups of family and friends, of heroes and villains, and also of actors in some of my favourite character performances. I'd forgotten that I'd included this section. But it makes sense. I prize character acting highly enough to feature it in a portrait of my life.

But what is it, character acting? And do I mean the same thing as other people?

In my childhood, there was a distinguished British actress called Margaret Rutherford, whose work I saw in the cinema (or bioscope, as it was known in South Africa). She was always very charismatic and funny: as Miss Prism in *The Importance of Being Earnest*, Madam Arcati in *Blithe Spirit* and Miss Marple in *Murder Most Foul*. Stout, white-haired, with popping eyes and quivering jowels, she was no one's idea of a film star, so she was politely referred to as a character actress. This was generally the case, even in the actors' directory, *Spotlight*: the beautiful people were listed as Leading Actors, the rest as Character Actors. But this is a nonsense, surely? I think the term 'character acting' refers to the powers of transformation. Margaret Rutherford had none whatever. Nor did you want her to have. You wanted her to be exactly the same glorious presence that she was in her last film. She was the ultimate Personality Actress.

In my adulthood, there has been Meryl Streep. She is the ultimate Character Actress. Her powers of transformation are phenomenal. She is totally convincing as the Danish farm-owner in *Out of Africa*, the Polish Holocaust survivor in *Sophie's Choice*, and the British Prime Minister in *The Iron Lady*. But she brings much more than a talent for mimicry to her roles, she brings her soul. This is crucial. Her characters may be vocally and physically different to herself, but shining through is her own spirit. It's a remarkable combination. It's the best acting I know.

Meanwhile, in terms of my own character-acting challenge, Falstaff, I may have accepted the part, but I notice I'm still not comfortable saying it aloud, saying it to other people. I'm nervous of glimpsing a look of incredulity in their eyes. So when I'm asked what I'm doing next, I tend to mumble something about hoping that *Hysteria* might have a future life... [*Photo insert, page 2, Character Acting*]

Monday 8 April

New York.

We're here for an RSC double whammy. In this one week, *Matilda* opens on Broadway, and Greg's production of *Julius Caesar* opens at BAM (Brooklyn Academy of Music).

We're staying on the south end of Central Park, at the Essex House Hotel, where I had a condominium during the Broadway run of *Primo*. We've just got a room for this visit, but it has the same spectacular view. The entire length of the Park stretches out below – it's like a runway, and you're coming in to land. From up here, the trees looked grey and wintry, but when we went downstairs, we found that the day was in fact rather warm and sunny. Greg needs a new jacket for all the public events coming up, so we strolled down to Bergdorf Goodman. Found a beautiful jacket – dark blue-black with a lighter blue fleck – and were impressed that they could do the alterations in time for his afternoon appointments: a round of press and TV interviews.

At 3.30 p.m., looking very smart in the jacket, he set off from the room. A moment later, rang from the lobby, to tell me that the publicist had asked what he was going to say about Margaret Thatcher.

He said why. The man said because she's died. As a visiting Brit of note, Greg would be invited to comment.

'I'll keep it short,' Greg said to me; 'I'll just say she was no friend to the Arts.'

I smiled, remembering how a few years earlier he refused to shake her hand. We were the guests of the late Bob Alexander (then RSC Chairman) at a dinner in Middle Temple, and the Thatchers were there too. Bob offered to introduce us. Greg said absolutely not, while I, who'd hated her when she was in power, now thought it would be interesting. I found her surrounded by young Tory fans. They asked her about the new leader, Iain Duncan Smith, and she answered diplomatically, being very positive about him. Emboldened by my glass of wine, I said, 'But you see, in my profession, there are leading players and supporting players – it's all to do with charisma – and you had it, you were undoubtedly a leading player, and he hasn't got it, he's a supporting player.' Torn between my flattery and her need to support Duncan Smith, she went quiet for a moment. I regard that as quite an achievement. I silenced Margaret Thatcher.

Evening. Another great view of the Park, now from a sumptuous apartment on the west side: a dinner hosted by one of BAM's biggest sponsors. I talked to the Shakespeare scholar James Shapiro, who sits on the RSC Board. He said that when he was a student, he admired my performance as Richard III, which was flattering to hear. He spoke passionately about Shakespeare, but with a streetwise New York spin: 'All my fellow students were taking drugs at the time, but I tell you, man, Shakespeare was my drug – I couldn't find any better high than Shakespeare!'

In Greg's speech to the guests, he explained why he'd set *Caesar* in Africa: it's a popular play on that continent, and Julius Nyerere (the first President of Tanzania after independence) even translated it into Swahili. Greg also mentioned the Robben Island Shakespeare. This was an edition of the *Collected Works* disguised as a Hindu prayer book, which was passed among the prisoners, some of whom signed their favourite passages. Mandela's choice was Caesar's speech, which begins, 'Cowards die many times before their deaths/ The valiant never taste of death but once.' (The Robben Island Shakespeare has become quite a famous book, and Greg and I are proud to have been part of discovering it: we heard about it in South Africa, and helped to bring it to Stratford for the Complete Works Festival in 2006.)

Thursday 11 April

A night of complete craziness, or, to put it another way, the opening of a Broadway musical.

Although *Matilda* was part of Michael Boyd's regime – and he was here tonight – it still fell to Greg to front the RSC, along with his Executive Director Catherine Mallyon. Her partner is Susan Foster (Director of Fundraising for the National Trust), and she and I did a lot of bonding as we followed Greg and Catherine about; we called ourselves 'the pretty young things on their arms'. When it came to the red-carpet moment, with Greg and I posing together on one side and Catherine and Susan on the other, I think the photographers were a teeny bit confused.

Inside the theatre, the Shubert, there was chaos. The audience only seemed interested in itself. Wouldn't stop talking, wouldn't sit down. The performance was meant to start at 6.30, but it was closer to 7 when it finally got going.

I never saw the show in the UK, so was surprised by everything. Particularly the anarchy. I laughed so much it was embarrassing – as though my tear ducts had become incontinent. Actually, my tears weren't just of joy – it was also very moving to see the children per-form with that phenomenal stage energy and expertise which is quintessentially *Broadway*. The nine-year-old girl playing Matilda – there are four of them alternating the role, and they just tossed a coin to decide who played tonight – was possessed of such calm confi-dence that it was almost as extraordinary as her character's super-intelligence. The cast achieved a brilliant cartoon style, and they were all-new, all-American – except for Bertie Carvel as Miss Trunchbull. He was even better than everyone has said. Facially, an eerie resemblance to Anthony Hopkins in *Silence of the Lambs*, and the body a glorious shape: a neckless, pumped-up, weightlifter's torso set atop long, quite slender legs. Best of all was his/her inner life: a psychopath on the verge of a nervous breakdown.

This was superb character acting. I didn't realise quite how superb till I met him afterwards: a handsome, thirty-something guy. It seems bizarre that he should have even been considered for the part, even more bizarre than me as Falstaff.

The post-show party was as out-of-control as the audience in the theatre: hundreds of people milling about in a vast room, swarming around the food tables, queuing at the bars. No special treatment for the RSC – not for Chairman Nigel Hugill, not for Deputy Chair Susie Sainsbury – we all had to just throw ourselves into the scrum.

Then suddenly someone ran up to Greg with *The New York Times* review on their iPhone. In this city, it's the only really important paper, and here was a rave, a mega-rave. Amazing. Within the space of just a few hours, we'd seen the show and got the verdict. And it's a hit. It'll run for years, it'll tour the world, it'll be filmed. And be a nice little earner for the RSC.

I said to Mike Boyd, 'This is a great way for you to finish.'

He said, 'And for Greg to start.'

It's true. Although Greg had little to do with it, he'll certainly benefit from this triumph.

As we were leaving, we popped into what was called The War Room, and stood at the back. A group of producers (including the RSC's Denise Wood), financial backers, and marketing folk were seated at a long table, discussing the next phase: advertising strategies, which quotes to use, etc. There was no air of celebration, no joy. Just a hard-nosed, slightly exhausted concentration. The room's nickname was appropriate. These people weren't planning the invasion of North Korea, just the future of a Broadway show – but the atmosphere was almost as intense.

Saturday 13 April

Compared to *Matilda*, *Caesar*'s opening at BAM tonight was an extremely civilised affair. The show was playing the smaller of their two main auditoria, the beautifully battered Harvey Theatre. Michael Vale's set of a crumbling concrete African stadium sat splendidly in this space. The show was on great form, and I've never seen the post-assassination sequence so dangerous. The conspirators had summoned up the courage to do the deed, but now what? Their adrenalin threatened to spiral out of control. When Mark Antony came on, it got worse. Anyone could have stabbed anyone. As Antony, Ray Fearon gave a thrilling display of Shakespeare acting: that perfect combination of verse technique and real passion. At the end of the show, the audience stood and cheered. I was moved. Greg was too, but covered it, saying, 'Oh, New York audiences stand for anything!'

Afterwards, I was required to join the other RSC folk in schmoozing the party guests: wealthy and powerful people who are American Friends of the RSC or BAM sponsors. I fell into conversation with one lady, who asked what I was doing next for the company. I made the mistake of telling her. She exclaimed:

'Falstaff? Oh no, I can't see that. You don't look right.'

I said, 'Well, watch this space,' (which was quite witty, actually) instead of kicking her arse. People talk to actors in a way they'd never dream of doing to other professions. Imagine saying to a doctor or lawyer, 'You don't look right for this job.'

Anyway, someone has said it aloud, the thing I most didn't want to hear, and it's fine, I'm still standing.

Sunday 14 April

The *Hobbit* script pages have finally arrived.

This has been quite a saga. On Thursday Nick Forgacs rang from my agents, saying that I'd been offered a part in *Hobbit 2*. They filmed most of it last year, but this was a new, extra sequence. Nick wasn't able to tell me much, other than that the character was called Thrain, he was King of the Dwarves, all his scenes were with Gandalf (Ian McKellen), and it would mean a couple of weeks in New Zealand. The film people couldn't show me the whole script – this was highly confidential – but my scenes would be conveyed to the hotel. However, the envelope couldn't just be left at the desk, it had to be handed over in person.

The drop-off was arranged for 10.30 this morning. Feeling like I was a spy in a movie, I went down to the lobby, and scanned the people there with an uncertain eye. Who was I to look for? Then a young woman suddenly came over, and handed me the envelope. We said no more than hello and goodbye.

Now I'm back in the room. There are about fifteen pages, each with my name stamped heavily across it (making some of the dialogue difficult to read) – it ensures that if any of this material was ever revealed publicly I could immediately be identified as the mole, the traitor.

After all this real-life drama, the scenes themselves are rather
straightforward. But I'm not sure if it's safe to reveal their content
even here. What if this diary was stolen?

Anyway, it doesn't really matter. The role is quite strong and I'll
be playing opposite Ian. The rest all comes down to how little time
it'll take to do, and how much money they'll pay.

My attitude to these film cameos is completely different to my theatre work. If you're playing a big leading role on stage, you have to
share the responsibility for the whole thing. If you're appearing
briefly in a film, your only responsibility is to do the little job effi-
ciently. But these same little jobs make it possible for me to do plays
which I'm passionate about in theatres that don't pay much, like the
Sheffield Crucible (*Enemy of the People*), the Kilburn Tricycle (*Broken Glass*), and Bath Theatre Royal (*Hysteria*).

Sunday brunch is one of New York's special pleasures. We had ours
at the Russian Tea Room just behind the hotel. An unexpected conversation took place.

I began tentatively: 'Listen… I've been thinking about the *Henries*… and I've had this idea… it's probably crazy… but I'm going
to say it anyway.'

Greg leaned forward over his caviar blinis, frowning but amused.

I carried on: 'What about a modern-dress production?'

There was a pause, then Greg said: 'Good heavens, I've been
thinking exactly the same thing.'

'Good heavens,' I echoed; 'I was sure you'd say it was completely
impossible. With these of all plays.'

'Yes, and maybe it is, but… I'm quite drawn to the idea.'

'Well, from my point of view it changes everything. I mean, for
Falstaff. If he doesn't have to look like some Toby jug from the sou-
venir shop, but… I don't know, a kind of British version of a Vietnam
vet. With a ponytail and bandana, an earring, big scruffy beard…
this battle-crazed old guy gone to ruin. I mean, it would be such an
original interpretation that the whole question of why *I'm* playing
it… well, it would just cease to be. I'm playing it because this is the
way we're playing the production. And the perfect Falstaff actor –
whoever that is – might not be able to play him like this. But I can.'

We talked about how it would affect other characters, pictured this
or that scene in a modern context, then went quiet, almost holding

our breath, both filled with the same thought: is this a good or bad idea? They're sometimes difficult to tell apart.

Greg said in a quiet, sensible tone, 'Well... let's keep thinking about it.'

'Right,' I replied; 'But I just have to say – this is very exciting!'

Saturday 20 April

Stratford-upon-Avon.

One of those mornings. I walked into the front room at Avonside, and had to stagger back, shielding my eyes. Sunlight was blazing on the river, beaming through our windows, bouncing off every wall. Perfect weather. It's Shakespeare's birthday celebrations today.

This begins with a parade through town. Taking part are local civic dignitaries, ambassadors or cultural attachés from every country in the world, scholars from the Shakespeare Institute and Birthplace Trust, and many others. The assembly point is outside the Town Hall at the top of Sheep Street. Prefects from KES were leading the various groups – we fell in behind the one holding the RSC placard. Catherine Mallyon was there too, with partner Susan, and as we set off we realised that, like on the red carpet for *Matilda* in New York, the RSC was being fronted by two people in same-sex relationships – a first for this time-honoured procession, I bet. A tiny, quiet bit of history being made.

There was a long wait on Bridge Street while flags were unfurled from every lamp post – Greg doing his RSC duty – and brass bands marched up and down. Then they led us through town, to Trinity Church, where we laid flowers on Shakespeare's grave.

The whole affair is quaint and slow, essentially English, and rather touching. In today's bright sunshine, there we all were, dressed in our smart clothes, some with hats and sunglasses, chatting about this and that as we strolled along to the bands' tunes, participating in a little country-town ritual, which happens to be honouring one of the most universally famous figures of all time.

The big lunch is next, but this has become a problem. There are so many speeches and toasts that the meal has been known to drag on for five hours, and leave guests dazed with Shakespeare-overkill. So this year, a new format is being tried. Two of the main events – the Toast to the Immortal Bard and the presentation of the Pragnell Prize – are happening first, at a different location. KES. We were given glasses of champagne as we arrived, then climbed upstairs to Shakespeare's schoolroom.

Here Margaret Drabble gave the Toast. It came as a surprise to learn that she had been 'a spear carrier' (her words) with the RSC in the early sixties, understudying both Judi Dench as Titania in Peter Hall's *Midsummer Night's Dream*, and Diana Rigg as Cordelia in Peter Brook's famous *King Lear* (with Scofield). She said, 'I cannot exaggerate the importance to me, through later years, of the experience of being so close to Shakespeare on stage.'

The recipient of this year's Pragnell Prize (given for outstanding contribution to Shakespeare) was Simon Russell Beale. In his acceptance speech, Simon proved himself to be very skilled at this sort of thing: his style was relaxed, spontaneous, seeming almost absent-minded, fussing with his papers, and of course humorous. I particularly enjoyed his story about doing the annual play at his all-male school. Those boys who played women (Simon was Desdemona!) were taught to hold their thumbs in their palms; 'I don't think it made us more graceful and feminine – we just looked like lemurs!'

The lunch which followed was not in its usual location – a marquee in the Bancroft Gardens – but in the Rooftop Restaurant at the theatre. We were seated next to Simon. I had decided not to mention that I was going to play Falstaff, but Greg did, almost immediately. Simon gave a little, non-committal smile and nodded. More than anyone, he knows about casting-against-type. The idea of him playing Hamlet seemed very far-fetched, yet it became one of his most acclaimed performances.

We talked about his Falstaff in the BBC TV film. Greg asked him if playing it to a theatre audience might have changed his way of doing it. He thought it might – their laughter would have shifted the tone – but he remained committed to the idea that Falstaff is haunted by death from the start. Now that I knew the part better, I disagreed – but didn't say so.

Anyway, Falstaff was past history for Simon. He had his sights on the next one – later this year he's playing Lear at the National, directed by Sam Mendes.

Friday 10 May

London.

I've been having problems in my lower back – a feeling of my hips being locked – and with the long flight to New Zealand coming up, decided to finally get it sorted. Went to Dr Ralph Rogers in Harley Street. He's an orthopaedic specialist, who deals with sports injuries. This kind of doctor is very useful for performers: like sportsmen, we need fast, and sometimes unconventional cures. He gave me some injections in the spine. Quite painful, but guaranteed to help, he assured me. Will have another treatment or two before the flight in a fortnight.

Back at home, thrilling news. *Hysteria* is back in the picture. The idea of a Broadway production fell away, like the West End transfer before it, but now there's an offer to do it at Hampstead Theatre. Perfect. In every way. It's just a mile or so from where the play is set, in Freud's last home at 20 Maresfield Gardens, now the Freud Museum. And it's a theatre where I've had a series of special experiences (Mike Leigh's *Goose-Pimples*, my one-man show *Primo*, my play *The Giant*). Rehearsals will be in August (their length dependent on which other members of the Bath cast want to do it), and it'll have a decent run till October. I feel excited and pleased. *Hysteria* gets its London showing after all, but in a small space, which should be packed. And as a job, it neatly fills the gap between *The Hobbit* and the *Henries*. Emailed Terry Johnson to express my delight.

Wednesday 29 May

New Zealand. Wellington. *The Hobbit* film studios.

I finally get the chance to say it to Ian McKellen's face:

'It's all your fault.'

'What is?'

'Me playing Falstaff. You suggested it.'

'Ah,' he says absently; 'Did I?'

We're in Ian's tent (where he waits between camera set-ups) in an area next to the sound stage. He is dressed and made up as Gandalf, and I as this character called Thrain. I am wearing facial prosthetics which take three and a half hours to apply each day, and which transform me so completely – into a big-nosed, big-chinned, big-eared, wrinkled, scarred, old Dwarf King – that when this movie comes out, I defy anyone to say whether it's me or Meryl Streep in the role. This is character acting which has nothing to do with the actor: it's the creation of the art director and make-up artist.

Anyway, although Ian has only a vague memory of suggesting me for Falstaff, he's very encouraging about me playing it: 'That part needs either a great clown or a leading actor with a feel for comedy. Which I think people would say both you and I are.'

'So why did you turn it down?' I ask.

'I've never really got Falstaff's humour,' he replies.

Here we are again – the humour. I don't actually see how a great clown (like George Robey, who played it in 1935) could pull it off. There's so much more to Falstaff than the laughs.

Ian says there was a moment a few years ago when he became tempted to play Falstaff – in a gay relationship with Hal. But he went to see a student production which tried this interpretation, and realised it didn't work.

No, absolutely not. The Falstaff/Hal relationship has to be father/son. The play makes Falstaff Hal's surrogate father – albeit the wildest, least conventional parent-figure imaginable – in stark contrast to Hal's real father, the King.

Ian goes on to tell me that when he was at Cambridge, his first success as an actor was as Justice Shallow in *Part II*. He was tutored in it by John Barton, very strictly, line by line, and to this day still remembers John emphasising the importance of the line, 'Nay, you shall see mine orchard' – saying how it conjured up a little patch of trees in golden sunlight, a little picture of England. Now Ian does an impersonation of his twenty-year-old self doing the speech, and I laugh – I can hear both him and John Barton in the delivery.

We're summoned to do the next scene. As a director, Peter Jackson is open and accessible, but, wearing slightly crumpled clothes and permanently clutching a mug of herbal tea, he also has the air of a man in the grip of a particular obsession – it's called making a blockbuster. It's extraordinary – the one-man film industry that he's built. He has created so much employment in New Zealand, and so enhanced its international profile, that they offered to rename Wellington Airport after him – but he declined. When we met last week, I was talking about growing up in South Africa, and mentioned that anyone interested in the arts always wanted to escape to that mythical place called Overseas. He said the same syndrome was true here, but he never felt that way. No – instead he's brought Overseas *here*.

His relationship with Ian is effortless. Of course it is. This is their fifth film together. As Ian says affectionately, 'I've been playing this fucking part for the whole of this fucking century!'

Peter's work method is totally relaxed. Virtually no rehearsal. You do a rough block-through, and then he starts shooting on what he calls rolling takes: one after the other, without shouts of 'Action' or 'Cut', just a few notes from him in between. (There's no expensive film stock being consumed; the digital stuff costs nothing.) So you create the scene while filming it, rather than trying to recapture what you did on a specially good rehearsal or take.

Because the dwarves have to be smaller than Gandalf, Peter employs several devices. Sometimes the camera angle is enough, or Ian stands on a box, and he and I can still play the scene together. At other times, the scale doubles are brought in. Ian has a seven-foot scale double called Paul (in real life, a local policeman), and I have a three-foot scale double called Kieren. Both are costumed and made up to look like us, and in some close shots I'll be reaching up to Paul's arm, or Ian will looking down to Kieren.

At times it's quite surreal. At lunch, in the huge canteen tent on the studio lot, you'll see the other dwarves – actors I know, like Ken Stott, Jimmy Nesbitt, Richard Armitage – in their prosthetics and body suits, sitting next to crew members in their ordinary clothes, and next to them the scale doubles. On my first few days, it wasn't only severe jet lag that made me feel I'd landed on Mars.

Sunday 2 June

I'm hopeless at being away on location. I'm no good at either social-ising or exploring, so when I'm not filming, I tend to stay holed up in my hotel, eating from the room-service menu, or sometimes ven-turing out to a restaurant.

'I take a book along,' I told Greg on the phone; 'And I don't feel lonely – but I know I *look* lonely.'

'Why don't you find your book amusing?' he suggested; 'And laugh occasionally, so people can see you're okay.'

'Because then I won't only look lonely, I'll look mad.'

The hotel, The Museum, is situated on the harbour, and there are attractive walks along the quayside, leading to an area not unlike Cape Town's Waterfront, with shops and restaurants. But the weather isn't great: we're going into New Zealand's winter, and the wind can be formidable – horizontal at times, I'm told.

Luckily, I've got a work project to occupy me during the long days in my hotel room. Cutting the *Henries*; i.e. reducing the text to a reasonable running time (about two and a half hours per play). This is something I first did with Terry Hands, when we decided to condense the two parts of *Tamburlaine the Great* into one: as, respectively, director and leading actor, we each did a cut separately, then met to compare and contrast. Greg and I have continued the tradition on our shows together.

This is a very enjoyable, learning process. Before you can cut a scene – I'm only doing the Falstaff ones – you have to really understand it. So I pore over the notes in the two editions I've brought with me, the RSC and the Arden, and then mark possible cuts – using pencil – in the scripts which the literary department has provided in A4 format. It's a terrific way of getting to know a play (or plays).

And it led to this conversation on the phone today:

Me: You know the idea we had in New York about a modern-dress production – it doesn't work, does it?

Greg: Carry on – I've been rereading them too – but carry on.

Me: Well, right from the early scenes... at Gad's Hill, Falstaff can't do without his horse... then he's been hacking his sword and his buckler... and a hundred other things... it's the whole atmosphere of the plays... they're like a love letter to an earlier England...

Greg: And it's not Henry IV's England – it's Elizabethan England, it's Shakespeare's England.

Me: Yes. It's what an audience expects from these plays... it's what *I* expect when I go to them... *I'd* be disappointed by a modern-dress production.

Greg: I totally agree.

We were in accord once again. But the exercise was valid, I believe. We proposed a modern-dress production, we examined the idea in more detail, we realised it didn't work, and now we'll revert to a period production. But Greg thought we could still incorporate some of the things which inspired us about a modern version. Like Falstaff as a Vietnam vet. There'll be ways of suggesting that.

There's an eleven-hour time difference between the UK and New Zealand. This phone call was happening on Saturday night for Greg, Sunday morning for me. All quite confusing. I got caught out last week, when Greg began a call by saying, 'Can I just thank you for the last twenty-six years.' Our anniversary! I knew that our twenty-sixth was on the 26th of May, but had no idea when the 26th of May was.

Anyway, when we finished today's call, I worked for about eight hours on the scripts, excited by our new concept of doing the plays old. Then I gradually ran out of energy, and sat there with a glass of wine, while outside my window with its wide view of the bay and harbour, day turned to night. I thought about going out to a restaurant, and then just dialled room service again...

I can't wait to go home.

Friday 14 June

Stratford-upon-Avon.

My birthday. My God, there was a Beatles song about being unimaginably old: 'When I'm Sixty-Four'. And that's me today.

Sunday 23 June

Over the last three days, I've been watching a unique performance of *Midsummer Night's Dream*. It's an RSC project with Google+: the play performed in three sections, each corresponding to the time scheme in the story, and with a lot of social-media activity surrounding the event: filming it, a video-diary room, and so on.

Greg directed, and managed to collect a cast together who had all played their parts before, either in his own production (like Joe Dixon as Bottom) or in others. This enabled them to rehearse in just one week.

It began on Friday evening, with the opening scenes, which introduce the Lovers, the Mechanicals, and the Fairies. This was in the Ashcroft Room, the huge, beautiful rehearsal space above the Swan Theatre. The audience sat in a circle, the actors wore their own clothes, and there were no lighting or sound effects. The piece was all the better for it: just the words conjuring up fantastical things, the play itself. I was next to Ciss Berry, the RSC's legendary voice guru. She's eighty-seven now, physically a bit frail, using a stick, but her mind is as bright as ever. 'The sexual imagery in the language!' she said, as excited as a teenager discovering it for the first time. The cast were splendid, and Joe Dixon so good that I got into one of my weeping-with-laughter states, with incontinent tear ducts.

I was hooked. Couldn't wait for the next instalment, though I'd previously said I wasn't sure I'd be able to manage it.

Because this took place at 2.30 a.m. on Sunday morning. The main body of the play: in the woods, in the middle of the night. Greg and I slept for a few hours beforehand, but the actors hadn't, and looked a bit dazed. And now they had to *work*. They needn't have worried. There was a special energy in the packed Ashcroft Room – everyone had made such an effort to be here – and both the performers and the audience just got intoxicated on Shakespeare. Like last night, the utter simplicity of the exercise – no costumes, no effects – turned it into the most magical *Dream* I've ever seen. And of course the circumstances made it genuinely dreamlike. Never more so than when the black outside the windows slowly turned to blue, and as Puck said, 'I do hear the morning lark,' the dawn chorus started up – as if cued by the stage manager. By the time we got to the end of tonight's section, which was Bottom's waking-up speech – 'I have had a most rare vision' – we all knew what he meant.

Out onto the Ashcroft terrace we went, for Buck's Fizz, bacon butties, and the quiet spectacle of Stratford, the river, the spire of Holy Trinity, gradually taking shape out of the surrounding darkness. We all looked strangely aged – well, we never normally see one another at 5 a.m. – but beautifully so, as if graced by something special. Then Greg and I walked back to Avonside, marvelling at what he called 'the oyster colours' of sunrise – greys and pinks – and collapsed into bed.

And now, at 11.30 p.m. on Sunday, we're assembled for the last part. This is taking place in the open air, in the Dell next to the church. There was a rainstorm earlier, thumping down in big silvery sheets on the river, and we held our breath. But it cleared quickly, and now the sky is clear, with an amazing moon, known as a supermoon – enormous, thick and orange – perfect for tonight, which is officially Midsummer.

The audience are in darkness, seated on blankets on the grassy bank, while the actors are on a little rise, lit by flaming torches, with the silhouette of trees and the bright disc of *that* moon behind them. They do Act Five: the Mechanicals performing *Pyramus and Thisbe* to the court. This is the funniest thing in all of Shakespeare's Comedies, and tonight's cast do it hilariously.

There was one last surprise for us all. Just before Theseus says the line, 'The iron tongue of midnight hath told twelve', the bells in the church alongside us begin to chime. (This *was* cued by the stage manager.) What a way to end.

I have to admit that when Greg first outlined the idea of this *Dream* to me, I found it a bit odd, a bit unnecessary. But I was wrong. I heard the play afresh this weekend, and rejoiced in it all over again.

As we're saying our goodbyes, I give Joe Dixon a hug: 'One of the best things in the world is to see a great performance of a great Shakespeare role. So thank you.'

He's chuffed, and says, 'And which of them will you be doing next?'

I smile for a long moment, as it occurs that *he* could play Falstaff, then I mutter, 'Oh, I dunno' – and change the subject.

Monday 1 July

Southern France.

When Greg got The Job, people's first response to me was odd. They wished me luck. Me, not Greg. I checked with the partners of previous Artistic Directors – Joanna Pearce and Caroline Boyd – and both gave the same small smile and said the same thing: 'You'll see.' I braced myself, like someone who'd secretly been given forewarning of a tsunami, but at first nothing seemed to change in our lives. We're both workaholics, so it wasn't unusual to spend Saturday and Sunday mornings in our separate studies. Then Greg started doing the afternoons as well. He was waking earlier, to read through the growing stacks of manuscripts, memos and briefings. When we were in Stratford he'd have to go to London, and vice versa. And there was *the machine*. Greg has always said, 'There are three of us in this marriage – me, Tony and Tony's diary.' Well, now there was a fourth. Greg's iPad. Given to him by the RSC, and programmed by them, it gradually became permanently attached to his hands. Now even on Sunday evenings, with us flopped in front of the telly, I'd be watching a programme, and he'd be on the iPad.

All this, and he hasn't yet done his first production as Artistic Director. That's about to happen – *Richard II* with David Tennant. Anyone who's directed a play knows it's an all-consuming task. So he'll be doing that *and* The Job.

Luckily, there's his PA Jane Tassell – still determinedly finding and guarding time for a holiday.

This is one of them. Just a week, so we've not travelled far. France – on the coast between Nice and Monaco. We'll probably visit them both, but we'll mainly stay at the hotel, Cap Estel, an attractive pink, beige and cream mansion above the sea. Our room is on a corner, with two balconies and a tremendous view.

When we arrived yesterday, the weather was dull, and we were worried. It was bad back in England (of course it was – Wimbledon's on), but would it spoil our brief stay here?

Thankfully no. When we pushed open the big wooden shutters on our windows this morning, we found a perfect day outside. The Côte d'Azur presented us with three blues: the powder blue of the sky, the deep blue of the sea, the turquoise blue of the swimming pool.

The pool is where we've spent the morning, and now we're lunching at the garden restaurant. The food is good: a whole grilled sea bream between us and delicious rice flavoured with orange. And that most delightful of holiday treats: wine at lunchtime. And French wine at that. A well-chilled Chablis.

Greg obviously doesn't want to talk about work, but the *Henries* are far enough in the future to still seem more like pleasure.

'Who have you known like Falstaff?' he asks.

I think hard. 'Well… I suppose some of the actors in my first RSC season. Like Pete Postlethwaite. Be up all night at The Duck, on all sorts of things, then rehearse during the day, perform in the evening, and then do another all-nighter. It never affected his work, and he was tremendous company, at whatever stage of this sequence you caught him, a real-life force. Resting in peace now. But he wasn't the only one. There was a whole group of them. The Dirty Duckers. Don't know how they did it.'

'But, sorry, weren't you one of them?'

'Oh… just a junior member of the club.'

'An embryonic Falstaff. Maybe he's closer than you think.'

'Don't know what you mean!' I say, filling our glasses. 'And then there was Alf's pal…'

Alfred Bradley is one of our closest friends, a schoolteacher (English and Drama), now retired. When he was a schoolboy himself, one of his classmates was a chap whom I shall call Roger here. He grew into a rich and powerful figure, the managing director of one of the big supermarket chains. Before Greg and I got together, I met Roger a few times – through Alf – and he was truly Falstaffian (except that he was gay): fat, drank like a fish, booming voice, very charming, in a slightly overwhelming way. He also shared Falstaff's appetite for criminality, and, having got into serious financial trouble, fled the country, cutting all ties completely. Alf believed he'd chosen Thailand as his place of exile, and pictured him there living on a diet of booze and boys, now more of a crumpled, Graham Greene figure. But it was actually because Roger was a Tolkien fan, and through a Tolkien website, that Alf learned he had died last year.

As I describe Roger's excesses, Greg wrinkles his nose in distate.

'Ah-hah!' I say; 'Is Falstaff one of those characters we relish onstage, but wouldn't want to meet in real life? Like Richard III or Iago. Is he part of that syndrome?'

'No, not at all,' Greg replies; 'I'd be very happy to spend an evening with him in the pub. He'd be great fun.'

'As long as you were buying the drinks.'

After lunch, another holiday pleasure – a long siesta. And then we decide to revive ourselves with a dip in the sea; the hotel has a little private beach. It's very attractive. The wash of pebbles up and down the slope of the beach, and the water of the Mediterranean, which, when clean – like here – is pure pleasure.

Growing up next to the sea, and having little access to it these days, I miss it terribly, and value it hugely. On a hot, calm afternoon like today, the immense expanse of water is in benign mood, yet you still feel its power. I become totally diminished as I enter it – just a little object to be freshened, purified, washed through and through. I don't swim, I dip under and then surface, again and again, flopping about like an old seal, looking foolish I know (I've seen photographs), yet *completely* happy.

I splash over to Greg: 'Last weekend, I told Joe Dixon that one of the best things in the world is seeing a great Shakespeare performance.'

'Agreed.'

'I want to nominate another – bathing in a great sea.'

'Agreed!'

Monday 8 July

London.

Natasha Harwood has died – she's been ill for some time – and this morning is her funeral.

In recent years, Greg and I have become close to the Harwoods. Ironically, it was the failure of a show in the West End – Ronnie's play *Mahler's Conversion*, with Greg directing and me playing Mahler – and the outrage that we all felt about its treatment which led to us bonding. Greg has to be in Stratford today, so I'm here to represent both us and the family in South Africa: Ronnie is my mother's first cousin.

The funeral is held at the Carmelite Monastery in Kensington Church Street. The place is bedecked with white flowers, and packed. Some famous faces among the mourners: Albert Finney, Tom Stoppard, and Antonia Fraser (Harold Pinter and Ronnie were young actors in Donald Wolfit's company, and Natasha was a stage manager). The readings are done by Maggie Smith and Tom Courtenay. A choir sings beautifully. At the end, when they do Fauré's *Requiem*, to accompany the carrying-out of the coffin, everyone is crying. In the procession, Ronnie walks with his eyes closed.

Out on the pavement, in baking sunshine, I finally get to hug him. I say the Jewish thing: 'Long life.' He says, 'Yes, that's what we should all have – she was only seventy-five, you know.' And they were together for fifty-six of those years – 'a damn fine marriage' as he once said to me proudly. God, how can he breathe without her?

When I get to Stratford a few hours later, I hold on to Greg tightly.

Wednesday 10 July

Stratford-upon-Avon.

I can't believe it – I'm doing a photo shoot as Falstaff. This is getting serious. This is getting real.

It's for the RSC brochure – Spring 2014 – and brochures are little tyrannies, laws unto themselves, forever demanding attention long before it seems necessary.

We had to think of an image. Neither Greg nor I were keen to attempt a 'Falstaff look'. I'm growing my beard for Freud, but it's not nearly big enough for Falstaff yet, and the idea of putting on a wig from stock and some generalised padding was out of the question. Greg came up with an ingenious solution. In fact it's one we used before, for the *Cyrano de Bergerac* poster back in 1997. A distorting mirror. Previously, it was to provide Cyrano's nose – today, Falstaff's girth. A studio was set up in one of the Arden Street rehearsal rooms, and the mirror placed in front of the lights. Wearing my own clothes, I sat in front of it, on a bar stool, holding a glass of wine. So the image was a double portrait: me at my normal size plus me ballooning into a fat man.

The photographer was Sasha Gusov, a cheerfully eccentric Russian, extremely gifted at his craft (he gave us a book of his work), who kept up a giggling commentary as he took the shots: 'That's it, Tony, a bit more cheeky, brilliant, eyes more open, that's it, I'm liking this, more cheeky, brilliant, the best yet…' It was helpful because it made me laugh for real.

We'll have to be careful in the selection though. We can't just have a jolly Falstaff. Hopefully the mirror will add something else, something more complex.

Saturday 13 July

Stratford.

A picture of our life together:

Saturday afternoon. *Jazz Record Requests* on the radio. Our French windows opened wide to the sunny river. Me inside, standing in front of my easel, painting. Greg sitting on the patio, working on the script of *Richard II*. Both of us with glasses of our namesake drink: G&Ts.

My painting is of the actress Kathryn Hunter. I'm a big fan of her work, and her performances in *The Visit* (playing the rich lady Claire Zachanassian, on crutches) and in *Kafka's Monkey* (playing a monkey who's playing a man) are two of the most inventive pieces of character acting I've seen. When she was with the RSC in 2010, she let me sketch and photograph her doing a warm-up for *Kafka's Monkey*. I've done a series of drawings of it, and now this triptych in oils.

Kathryn Hunter warming up for "Kafka's Monkey"

Sunday 28 July

London.

I'm fitting in a small, low-budget film before *Hysteria*. It's called *War Book*. The script, by Jack Thorne, is strikingly original. A group of civil servants gather to 'rehearse' what might happen in the event of a nuclear war. It mostly takes place in one room – like *12 Angry Men* – yet is more gripping than most action films. The clever thing is that the apocalypse isn't really happening, so you don't have to try and create the massive drama, or even melodrama, of that, yet you get to imagine it in every grisly detail as the characters act out their daily meetings while the crisis develops. It's immensely unsettling.

My character, David, is the financial adviser (others are from the departments of health, security, and so on): he says very little for much of the film, and then has a huge, four-page speech towards the end, which influences the outcome. In terms of character acting, it's a minimalist job. He's a bit fussy, bit pedantic, bit reserved – very English.

Despite the fact that the pay is peanuts, the director Tom Harper has managed to get a crack cast, including Sophie Okonedo, Ben Chaplin, Kerry Fox and Shaun Evans. Everyone's doing it because the script is good, and you don't often get that in the movies.

The piece is as static as a stage play and as talkative as a radio play – yet it's on film, so has to be carefully learned. We had a week's rehearsal, and are halfway through the two-week shoot. This is in Brent Town Hall (which is deserted – they've moved elsewhere). Outside, the rest of the country is still enjoying the current heatwave, while we – both cast and crew – are crammed into a conference room, which grows increasingly airless and hot. Particularly if it's *your* close-up, and you've got a lot of technical jargon in your dialogue. The pressure of two cameras and all your fellow actors staring at you is breaking the strongest of spirits. And of course time is ticking away too. Unlike a normal film, there's no leeway, no contingency plan. We will finish next Friday, and guess what – that's when my big speech is scheduled.

Friday 2 August

Did my big speech. It was fine. Thank God. Or my theatre training.

Monday 5 August

How nice to start a job without any fear. It's simply a pleasure to be back with *Hysteria* again, and back at Hampstead again.

There's me and David Horowitz (playing Yahuda) from the Bath production, and two new members of the cast: Lydia Wilson as Jessica and Adrian Schiller as Dalí.

Our writer/director Terry Johnson tells us about the genesis of the play. He'd struggled with it for a couple of years, trying different versions: one was set on a train (when Freud fled the Nazis), another in Jung's lighthouse. 'Then I decided to do some research,' says Terry; 'I prefer it that way round, or it can get in the way.' He visited the Freud Museum (just up the road from where we're sitting in Hampstead's rehearsal space), and as he walked into Freud's study, the thought struck him: 'Now I know how to do the play – it has to take place in this room!'

Of course.

A room of dreams. Where patients would lie on the famous couch and disclose the secret stuff that bubbles up in their brains while they sleep. This was a place where you could take Freud's preoccupation with the unconscious and Dalí's passion for surrealism, those two dreamworlds, toss them into the air, and juggle with them.

'And best of all,' says Terry; 'That room in Maresfield Gardens is a *set*, it's not real, it's been reconstructed from his actual study in Vienna. It's an illusion!'

How very apt, how very Terry Johnson. [*Photo insert, page 3, 'Hysteria'*]

I have an odd history with Terry, and it's something of a miracle that we're working together at all, never mind so happily.

In 1999 I was cast as Sid James in Terry's play, *Cleo, Camping, Emmanuelle and Dick*. But after the first week of rehearsals, I had to leave. Terry (who was also directing) and I couldn't agree on whether we should do impersonations of the *Carry On* actors, or just play characters called Sid, Ken and Babs. It all worked out well in the end – Geoff Hutchings stepped in to play Sid, and did it much better than I could've – but at the time it was an unpleasant and tense situation. If I was Terry, I wouldn't have employed me again, but he offered Freud, we met and cleared the air, and it's turned into a terrific experience.

Something of a lesson to be learned there. This isn't a profession in which to make enemies. Everything tends to come round in the great whirligig of theatre...

Saturday 10 August

Most enjoyable morning. Greg and I sat at our kitchen table, comparing the cuts we've both made to *Part I* of the *Henries* (Falstaff scenes only), and through a process of approval, refusal, and sometimes bartering, created a version which will be called the Rehearsal Draft, and which I can start learning as soon as *Hysteria* has opened.

Over lunch, at The Draper's Arms in Barnsbury Street, we discussed a way of doing the first Falstaff/Hal scene. Maybe set in some bawdy house (brothel). Hal is in bed with a whore, and then what we think is a pile of old blankets stirs in one corner, and it's Falstaff: 'Now Hal, what time of day is it, lad?' The whore leaves, and the scene ensues.

But what is Hal wearing when he gets out of bed? Nothing? When we were considering a modern-dress production, we talked about how the real, current Prince Harry was photographed nude, partying in a Las Vegas hotel room. But Greg doesn't want to take this parallel too far – perhaps because the RSC's President, Prince Charles, has already booked to see the show. So – Hal will be wearing something. I'm relieved. I wasn't that crazy about my first appearance being upstaged by a naked young man.

It looks like Alex Hassell is going to play Hal. This is good news. Alex has always been Greg's first choice. They worked together on *Cardenio*. I remember seeing the first preview, and being knocked out by Alex. He had the dark beauty of the young Oliver Reed, the charisma of a rock star, and a real talent for classical acting.

Wednesday 14 August

Shakespeare's History Plays are still surprisingly controversial. The *Henries* upset scholars of the period – the portraits of both the King and Hal are inaccurate – and when I played Richard III, I was besieged by letters from the Richard III Society, chastising me for propagating Shakespeare's warped image of their hero. In September 2012 they helped to fund the excavation of Richard's skeleton from under a Leicester car park, and were disappointed to discover that he really was a hunchback. They'd always claimed that it was part of Shakespeare's distortion.

The point all these people can't grasp is this: history is history and drama is drama.

Hysteria shows Freud meeting Dalí. This did actually occur, but it was a brief, unremarkable encounter (apart from the fact that Dalí produced a few small sketches of Freud). In the play, however, the handshake between these two giants of the subconscious ignites a firework display of farce, drama and fantasy.

The role of Freud is a gift to a character actor, allowing him to play both the real man and a cartoon of him.

I read several of the biographies, but most useful was a documentary which the Freud Museum have in their shop: home movies of him in the last year of his life. You can see how powerful his brain is, even though his body is a shadow of its former self (because of the mouth cancer).

I love playing this combination: mental strength and physical frailty. But when we did the play last year, I remember a strange disparity developing. When I was in a scene, my body felt absolutely right: brittle-thin and wasted. But then I'd experience the constant disappointment of seeing myself in mirrors or production photos... no, my weight, my shape was all wrong! It didn't matter – nobody said verisimilitude was the name of the game – but it was nevertheless odd: that the feeling didn't correspond to the look. Acting plays mind games with you that are sometimes difficult to fathom.

On the other hand, a different side of Freud's physicality has become easier this time round. The play has a section of pure farce, and this requires the actors to adopt the high-speed dexterity of the form. In Bath, I could not reconcile Freud's age with the agility required, nor his gravitas with this new frivolity. But I was being too literal, I now realise. The whole piece is a dream, a death dream, a hallucination induced by the shot of morphine which the doctor gives him to aid his pain-free passing. Anything can happen, and does, and the actor simply has to go with it.

Easier said than done. But I'm more relaxed now, having experienced the play in performance. I *know* it works.

Friday 16 August

More news on the *Henries* casting. Jasper Britton is going to play King Henry. He's such a tremendous actor that I'm already excited to see what he's going to do with that tough, tough part. And Paola Dionisotti is interested in Mistress Quickly. Greg thinks she'll do it.

Tuesday 20 August

This is difficult – these four weeks of re-rehearsing *Hysteria*. The newcomers (Lydia and Adrian) need every minute of it, while the old hands (David and I) are struggling to find ways to use the time. Our double act works splendidly, but what more can we do with it? And there are no laughs in rehearsals. Always a tricky thing with comedy, but worse this time, after playing it in Bath and on tour. Those gales of laughter. Now it's as if there's something missing.

Thursday 22 August

I need some Falstaff stimulation. Greg suggested I read Kenneth Tynan's review of Ralph Richardson in the 1945 Old Vic production (with Olivier doing a spectacular double as Hotspur and Shallow). I hesitated at first. Because Richardson's performance is often referred to as one of those definitive interpretations of a Shakespeare role. But there's no such thing, I know that. It's what has allowed the plays to be done again and again, over four centuries. The great roles are greater than any one actor. So I plunged into Tynan's review, and his opening line immediately gave me hope:

'Richardson's Falstaff was not a *comic* performance: it was too rich and many-sided to be crammed into a single word.' He goes on: 'Here was a Falstaff whose principal attribute was not his fatness but his knighthood. He was Sir John first, and Falstaff second, and let every cock-a-hoop young dog beware.' There was a particular dignity to his movement: 'As the great belly moved, step followed step with great finesse lest it overtopple, the arms flapped fussily at the sides as if to paddle the body's bulk along.' And, interestingly, 'None of the usual epithets for Falstaff applied to Richardson: he was not often jovial, laughed seldom, belched never. In disgrace, he affected the mask of sulky schoolboy...' Tynan's description of the big moment at the end, when Hal rejects Falstaff, was enticing – Richardson kept his back to the audience during Hal's speech, then slowly turned – and it may be worth stealing.

I look at photos of him in the part. Bald wig, big white beard, rather bizarre flyaway moustache and eyebrows. Although only forty-three when he played it, the make-up turns him into the older Richardson whom I saw in the 1970s, still at the top of his game in

Ralph Richardson as Falstaff

those two superb double acts with Gielgud: *Home* and *No Man's Land*. I rejoiced in him. That 'Oh-h-h' sound – not unlike the Churchill dog in the TV advert who goes, 'Oh-h-h yes!' Richardson's voice didn't seem to come from the normal place, but then neither did his acting. In fact, he didn't act so much as show you his soul, and this was a most rare, most wonderful, and slightly batty thing. He said of Falstaff that he 'proceeds at his own chosen pace, like a gorgeous ceremonial Indian elephant'. In a way that sums up Richardson's own distinctive, unforgettable form of acting.

Monday 26 August

Greg's fear this morning – about starting *Richard II* – was touching to behold. If only his company could see what I saw (his whole being was smaller, weaker, paler). Or maybe not. Actors want directors to be Daddy, if not God: all-powerful and invincible. Anyway, needless to say, when he returned this evening, it was in triumph. The day had been a success, and compliments flowed from his cast – hardened veterans like Michael Pennington, Oliver Ford Davies, Jane Lapotaire – as well as his star, David Tennant.

Wednesday 4 September

The back of Hampstead Theatre overlooks a big bowl of lawn, with a water feature, and on hot days like today – we're having another heatwave – the grass is covered with sunbathers and picnickers. It's rather idyllic, very un-English, quite sexy.

The front of the theatre, however, induces different sensations in me. It faces the Central School of Drama. There's a flight of steps leading up to their entrance, and these same steps play a small but significant part in my history. A week after arriving from South Africa in July 1968, I auditioned at Central, and my mother filmed me with our home-movie camera as I went up the steps. She thought she was catching a moment of history – the start of a glorious career – but instead I came back into view disgraced. Central had turned me down smartly. It was a little baptism by fire, showing the reality of trying to become an actor in this country. At the time it shocked me badly. And it's incredible, forty-five years later, that the sight of those steps still sends a shiver down my spine.

Anyway, over the last couple of days, we've tech'd *Hysteria* so quickly, that we were able to have a dress rehearsal this afternoon, and then Terry gave us the evening off…! A precious thing when you're about to embark on a sustained period of eight shows a week.

Back at home, I found Greg in a happy mood too. They'd done their first proper read-through this afternoon (after a week and a half of paraphrasing the text), and the cast were firing on all cylinders. Beforehand, this morning, they did a company research trip to Westminster Abbey, to see Richard II's tomb.

'What will we do as research for the *Henries?*' I asked; 'All go to a pub and get pissed?'

Thursday 5 September

First preview of *Hysteria*.

Must say I felt a sense of pride – a character actor's pride – as I did the finishing touches to my Freud appearance in the dressing room. My weight might be wrong, but the rest was not bad at all. The wig, creating the balding, silver-haired dome of his head, the hour and a half of make-up, with my beard whitened, my features aged, and the ugly, cancerous mark on his right cheek. The round glasses, the grey-brown suit – very professorial – the shirt and tie carefully reproduced from photos of the actual man. One of these is stuck on my mirror. I touched it, made a little gesture in the direction of Maresfield Gardens, then went downstairs to the stage.

What a joy to have an audience again, and laughter again! It lifted the roof of Hampstead's little auditorium. David and I weren't really surprised, but Lydia and Adrian were amazed.

Lydia has an exceptional gift for emotional acting. In the course of the action, her character, Jessica, undergoes a session of analysis, which begins as play-acting, but then gradually overwhelms her. When Lydia did this breakdown for the first time in rehearsals, it was completely real, with real tears and real anguish. Afterwards, Terry and I said to one another how good it had been, and I remarked, 'Now all she has to do is repeat that again and again.' (The curse of theatre acting.) Well, she *does*. Every single time. Goes to that same raw place inside her. I don't know how.

And Adrian's Dalí is completely believable: comic and crazy, a genius and a pseud wrapped into one. There are very few actors who could walk that tightrope with such skill.

We're lucky. Our new cast is as strong as the first one. We're going to be okay…

Monday 9 September

Was planning to wait till *Hysteria* opened to the press before starting on my next big project: learning Falstaff. But suddenly there's no need to wait. Will start tomorrow…

Self as Voigt

Character Acting (2 details from "The Audience"):
Meryl Streep in "Sophie's Choice", Ian McKellen in "Othello", Marlon Brando in
"Godfather".

...Anthony Quinn in "Requiem for a Heavyweight", Charles Laughton in
"Hunchback of Notre Dame", Bette Davis in
"Baby Jane"

"Hysteria"

"Prospero and the Spirits"

Paola Dionisotti as Mistress Quickly

Ciss listening

"G & T at Avonside"

My Falstaff

3. All Those Lines

'How do you learn all those lines?'

This question is the one that the public most frequently ask of actors. We laugh about it, laugh at them for being so shallow – as though learning lines was the great mystery in acting.

Well, I've stopped laughing. It's an age thing. In recent years, I've started doing something which I'd have disapproved of before: learning all the lines *before* rehearsals begin. It's the only way now. How, as a younger actor – as one of the Dirty Duckers in Stratford in '82, partying all night, rehearsing all day, performing in the evening – how I found time to learn lines as well, I've absolutely no idea.

When you're young, it seems so straightforward: you learn the lines and that's that. But when you're older, you're aware of a series of tests and obstacles ahead, each of which will put pressure on you, and the lines will often be the first casualty. So...

You have to know them alone in your room.

You have to know them when you speak them aloud with the other actors.

You have to know them when the ante is upped in the rehearsal room (such as a run-through).

You have to know them in front of the first audience at the first preview.

You have to know them in front of the critics.

You have to know them on a wet Wednesday matinee three months later, when the house is thin and you're thinking about the shopping...

This morning, I carefully put out the things I'd need. This is in my painting studio in our London house, a rear basement room with a conservatory glass roof. I set my drawing board at an angle to the wall, and prop the script on it. I'll learn from our A4 version, but on the shelf at my side are two published editions – the RSC and the Arden – for reference.

And it's those published editions that are the most intimidating, those smart, scholarly paperbacks – two pairs for the two plays: I have to transfer rather a lot of the material from inside them to inside my brain.

How? Today, I'm like the most naive member of the public. *How will you learn all those lines?*

I begin with the first Falstaff/Hal scene (Act One, Scene Two). I say Falstaff's first line: 'Now Hal, what time of day is it, lad?' I say it again, and again, pacing round. I move on to his next line – 'Indeed, you come near me now, Hal...' – and I practise that. Then I try the two lines together – but I've already forgotten the first. I start again. And so – the process is under way.

To an actor, dialogue is like food. You hold it in your mouth, you taste it. If it's good dialogue the taste will be distinctive. If it's Shakespeare dialogue, the taste will be Michelin-starred. Falstaff's dialogue is immediately delicious: you're munching on a very rich pudding indeed, savoury rather than sweet, probably not good for your health, but irresistible.

If you're learning lines before rehearsals, you have to learn in neutral, in a way that won't cut off the creative choices that will happen when the director and other actors are involved. So I'm speaking Falstaff in my own voice, I'm not attempting any characterisation.

At the same time, I can't help noticing things about the man, and becoming drawn to certain ones. He's well-educated, I see (he knows about Phoebus, Diana, similes and iteration), and he's a thief, a highwayman. A gentleman rogue then? That breed of privileged, public-school Englishmen, who can be both monstrous and charming, both powerful and self-destructive. The kind that believe the world belongs to them. They can break the law – *it's only a bit of fun.* They can drink themselves senseless – *it's what we chaps do.* And they'd be totally at ease hanging out with the future King – *I'll teach him a thing or two.* This country is full of men like that. Maybe that's why Falstaff is so loved – he's so familiar.

When I finish the session, I realise I've been at it for three hours. God. Time flying like when I'm writing or painting. But this is acting. Which I love less. It's too much like hard and boring graft: doing a run of eight shows a week is a conveyor-belt job. Anyway, today's work was pure pleasure.

Wednesday 11 September

Came downstairs this morning, to find that Greg had left the new RSC brochure on the kitchen table for me to see. The cover has a picture of me from that photo shoot we did – sitting in front of the distorting mirror, ballooning into Falstaff. It has worked well – an excellent image.

I suddenly had a real sense of optimism. Which isn't like me at all. Anyway, there's *Hysteria*'s press night tomorrow: that'll bring some dread and danger back into my life…

Thursday 12 September

Press night. It went well. The audience was good, not great, just good, but, more importantly, the show was strong. Nice compliments afterwards from a trio of Michaels: Frayn, Attenborough, and Leigh. The latter had seen our Bath production as well.

He was very enthusiastic about me playing Falstaff, and asked how I was going to put on all the weight.

I replied, 'Luckily, all Falstaffs have to wear a fat suit.'

He said, twinkling, 'No, that's not good enough.'

I laughed: 'No of course – the Mike Leigh way would be to do it for real.'

'You did for *Goose-Pimples*.'

'Mike! I wore padding.'

'You put on weight as well.'

There's no arguing with him. As I looked round the party in the foyer, I had a sense of things coming full circle. The old Hampstead Theatre was where we first did *Goose-Pimples*, before it transferred to the Garrick. Marion Bailey was in that show, and now she is Mike's partner. Her former partner was Terry Johnson. (They have a daughter, an actress.) And just to add to the mix, Mike's ex, Alison Steadman, was here tonight too…!

Friday 13 September

Felt strangely tired and low this morning. Nothing to do with it being Friday the 13th, and Yom Kippur, and a miserable drizzly day. No, more to do with the pressure of yesterday's opening.

Wondered if I'd have the energy for line-learning. But, as always, creativity acted as a tonic, and as soon as I started my tiredness fell away. I looked at Falstaff's big soliloquy at the beginning of the Gad's Hill robbery (Act Two, Scene Two). What joy again – him complaining about the dishonesty of his fellow thieves. I suppose this is an example of the role's comic reputation. But I still refuse to be intimidated by it. He's not trying to be funny – he's genuinely outraged that the others have hidden his horse, and left him, an old, fat man, to walk.

Then I went over all the lines I've done this week. One of the main difficulties of line-learning is that you have to constantly revise, while also trying to move forward. Or rather, inch forward. Real progress is painfully slow, and, given my naturally impatient temperament, it's frustrating.

Also, Falstaff is written entirely in prose – apart from some rhyming couplets to end scenes – and this is, surprisingly, harder to learn than verse (there's music in iambic pentameter, which sticks in the brain like a tune).

At first, a big part seems impossibly big. And this is effectively two big parts.

Tuesday 17 September

Our *Hysteria* reviews have been excellent – one five star, the rest fours.

But you still can't please everyone.

During Jessica's breakdown tonight – with Lydia doing it for real, as always – an old lady got up from the front row, huffed and puffed her way up the stairs to the exit, and in that uncensored way which the elderly (and children) have, said loudly to the usher, 'I'm feeling sick, and this play is making me sicker!'

Thursday 19 September

After feeling rather grumpy yesterday – it was a matinee day, so no time for line-learning – my spirits were flying again this morning. Worked on the famous tavern scene (Act Two, Scene Four). Just the big speeches in the 'play within the play', when Falstaff and Hal take turns to be the king, interrogating his wayward son. Spent three hours on one and a half pages. As well as the joy of savouring the language, there's the joy of understanding it, 'translating' it into ordinary English. Greg has always said there's a closet clerk in me, and it's this fussy little chap who loves cross-checking the notes in the RSC and Arden editions, and then writing out the meaning of a word or phrase in pencil on the page opposite the text. There is the most delicious sensation – a taste in the mouth again – when you *make sense* of a difficult Shakespeare line, when you can speak it with the gist held inside it, but speak it effortlessly, not spelling it out but making it sound second nature. Then, even if the audience don't fully grasp it, they get some impression of it, a feeling of clarity, from your interpretation.

At other times, the language is as simple as can be, and then it's Shakespeare's melodic sense again that lifts your heart. Here's Falstaff's riff on himself: 'Sweet Jack Falstaff, kind Jack Falstaff, true Jack Falstaff, valiant Jack Falstaff, and therefore more valiant, being as he is old Jack Falstaff…' It's like African praise-singing.

I can't remember enjoying the exploration of a text as much as this before.

Falstaff is a gift.

I must thank Greg for it. I can forget to do things like that.

Monday 23 September

One of the pluses of working at Hampstead is that I can drive there, park in the car park across the road, and then after the performance I can be home in twenty minutes.

This afternoon, the traffic was so light I arrived early, and strolled round the big lawn behind the theatre. It brought to mind an image of Greg and me doing the same thing, but in a very different, very tense situation.

It was in November, 2007, during the previews of my play *The Giant*, which Greg directed. The storyline followed the carving of

"The Giant" (detail from "The Audience"): Michelangelo's David, with Stephen Hagan's head (playing Vito) and the statue's body

Michelangelo's *David*, with the artist using a young quarryman, Vito, as his model. The set was dominated by the colossal block of marble. This began in a horizontal position, was hoisted upright, and then gradually transformed into the famous statue.

It was the hoisting upright that was the problem.

Although not real stone, the block was heavy and cumbersome, and lifting it was difficult for Hampstead's limited stage machinery. Greg had turned this part of the action into a civic ceremony, and our composer, Paul Englishby, had written a tremendous Latin hymn which the whole cast belted out with full-throated power. But again and again – in the tech, in the dress rehearsal, in the previews – they would come to the end of the music, and the block still wasn't in place. For one member of the audience, the (relatively inexperienced) playwright, this was agony beyond belief.

So in the interval of the third preview, I grabbed Greg's arm, and said, 'Can we talk?' We walked round the big lawn. I said, 'Listen, we're going to have to cut the lifting of the block.'

'Everyone's doing their best,' he said quietly, trying to calm me. 'I know that.'

'And it'll get faster.'

'Well, maybe it will, maybe it won't. I don't think we can risk it. The whole play stops dead. The block's just going to have to be vertical from the start. I've been thinking about it for a few days, and I'm sure now. We're cutting the lift. Please.'

He thought deeply, then said, 'Well, I don't agree. But it's your play. I'll tell everyone at tech notes, and we'll work out how to restage it.'

'Thank you.'

I was so fraught I decided to miss the second half and go home. But first I had to have a quick drink with our guest for the evening, Richard Wilson (actor, director, and close friend). I found him in the pub opposite. He was enjoying the show immensely, he said, and then added, 'The best bit was the lifting of the block.'

'What?! But it takes for ever.'

'That's what I liked. It was so heavy – it made it so important, so real.'

'But... we've just been talking about cutting it.'

'Oh no, no,' he said in that certain way of his – no one can be more certain than Richard – 'No, you can't cut it. I won't allow you to. I promise you it holds, I promise you it works!'

I stared at him, gave a strange laugh, a kind of yelp, then charged back across the road, and found Greg as he was heading back into the auditorium: 'We're not cutting the lift!'

'What? Good. But why?'

'I'll explain later.'

'Fine. It's your play. We're not cutting the lift. But we will get it faster.'

'Thank you.'

'Not at all,' he said, smiling gently, as to one who was losing their marbles, then went into the theatre.

Richard Wilson being certain

Thursday 26 September

The weeks are flying by: learning Falstaff in the mornings, playing Freud in the evenings. The entire run of *Hysteria* has been sold out. There's a queue for returns at every performance. Very gratifying.

Wednesday 2 October

Message from Nick Forgacs at my agents. Peter Jackson wants to talk to me on the phone. This can only be bad news. Why else would he need to do it personally? I suppose Thrain has had to be reduced in the final cut of the movie. I don't care. There was never any glory to be got from it.

The photographer Stewart Hemley came to the theatre for a couple of hours before the matinee. I've commissioned him to create a record of the Freud make-up being applied, and then some portraits of the finished job. I'll use these as references for a triptych I'm planning to paint. Called *Three Jews*, it'll be self-portraits in the roles of Gellburg (*Broken Glass*), Jacob (*Travelling Light*), and Freud. I want to show the same face, an actor's face, being altered by make-up. I'll do this in my new studio in our new Stratford house. Becoming the Artistic Director of the RSC is like becoming Prime Minister or a vicar: you get a house with the job. But the building has bad subsidence, and is being extensively renovated at the moment; we probably won't be able to move in till next spring, after the *Henries* have opened.

Thursday 3 October

As things worked out, Peter Jackson didn't phone, but emailed. Thrain hasn't just been reduced, but cut altogether. Purely to do with the length of the film, and not my 'wonderful performance'. As I said, I don't care in any important way, but if I think of the waste of time – those days of flying, those hours of prosthetics – it's mind-boggling. Anyway, I can cry all the way to the bank; I still get paid in full. And so endeth my experience of blockbusters – on the cutting-room floor.

Saturday 12 October

The last two *Hysterias*. They went by quickly. At the end, Terry Johnson popped in to my dressing room to say goodbye. He seemed emotional; hard to tell – he keeps things under tight wraps. Anyway, I've grown very fond of him, and his play is one of the best modern plays I've ever done, and I'm so pleased that it ended like this, with a short, sold-out run, rather than struggling to survive in the West End (or whatever might have happened on Broadway). I find eight performances a week hard to do – of anything – so these few weeks were quite enough for me, perfect in fact.

A car was waiting to drive me to Stratford. On the way, I had a Marks and Spencer's picnic of sandwiches and two miniature bottles of wine. And then I was there, at Avonside, in the arms of my loved one, and he joined me in my traditional chant at the end of a run: 'Freedom, free-dom!'

Monday 14 October

Preview of *Richard II*. I'm prejudiced I know, but it was pretty damn good. Designer Stephen Brimson Lewis and Lighting Designer Tim Mitchell have created epic images on a deceptively simple set: a reflective floor, a huge, high curtain of delicate chain, a bridge which descends from the flies with the King, godlike, on the throne. Paul Englishby's music is beautiful. But it's the cast that are the real knockout. Greg has vowed to get leading actors back to the RSC, and in tonight's show, there were leading actors even in the *supporting* roles. Jane Lapotaire kicked off the evening with a blazing portrayal of grief as the Duchess of Gloucester, Michael Pennington did John of Gaunt's 'This England' speech better than I've ever heard it, and Oliver Ford Davies was so good as York that you wondered why the part wasn't more famous, more prized. Nigel Lindsay was terrific as Bolingbroke, a real *bloke*, and the perfect foil for David Tennant's Richard, who looked quite feminine, with long red hair and slinky gowns. It's a startling, striking interpretation. He is utterly vain, utterly narcissistic – almost alienating us – until things start to fall apart, and then he's like a man discovering himself, and the world, for the first time. Very vulnerable, very moving – in the 'hollow crown' speech, and in prison: 'I wasted time and now doth time waste me.' At the end, there was a standing ovation.

Wednesday 16 October

I'm sitting in the office of the Artistic Director of the RSC, and it's Greg's office. I still can't get over this fact. On one wall, he's put up my big picture (done with coloured pencil on canvas) from the 2007 *Tempest* that I was in: a co-production between Cape Town's Baxter Theatre and the RSC. Called *Prospero and the Spirits* it shows me in the role, but sitting backstage in front of a costume rail, from which hang the fantastical African puppets that were used to create the spirit world. It's all quite shadowy, except for a bottle of mineral water at my feet – this glows brightly. It's the real source of magic for an actor playing one of Shakespeare's biggies.

We're here for the first *Henry IV* design chat-through with Stephen Brimson Lewis. He and Greg want the production to look very different from Richard – that's glittering and metallic, this needs to be more earthy, maybe a peat floor, maybe wooden walls.

In terms of Falstaff's look, I said, 'It just needs to be the best fat suit in the world.' Stephen knew exactly which people to go to. He explained that they make the suit in separate sections, each weighted, so that they move like flesh and not padding, which tends to bulk together when you sit, and you end up looking like there's a pillow stuck up your front. I mentioned the importance of matching the head to the body. I said, 'Probably a big beard, big hair, like that – ' pointing to the Prospero picture. Stephen looked at it: 'Yes, your whole head is bigger.' I said, 'The neck is often a giveaway when actors wear fat suits, the join point, we'll have to wear something round my neck. And what about my hands...?' I told them about the prosthetic hands I wore in *The Hobbit*: they went on like long gloves, and although unpleasant to wear – hot and clammy – they looked effective. Stephen didn't think it was necessary: 'Fat people often have delicate hands. And their legs can be surprisingly thin.' I like Stephen's eye for detail. [*Photo insert, page 4, 'Prospero and the Spirits'*]

At one point, he talked about balancing up the demands of comedy and realism. I said there needn't be any conflict. Explained that I'm not going to approach it as a comic role, but as a character role. 'So the fat suit simply needs to make me look as fat as *I* could feasibly be.'

After the meeting, walking back to Avonside, I thought again about these categories, Comedy, Drama, Tragedy. Why do they persist in our heads? Hasn't modern playwriting swept away the divides? (I expect to laugh and cry when I see Beckett, Miller, Stoppard.) In fact, Shakespeare himself swept them away. I got some great laughs as Macbeth, Leontes, Titus, even Prospero, and as for Richard III, he brought the house down when, at the end of the Lady Anne scene, he turned to the audience, and asked, 'Was ever woman in this humour wooed?'

Thursday 17 October

Press night of *Richard II*. The cast rose to concert pitch – which is very difficult to achieve on demand – and the show was quite simply superb.

At the party afterwards, I bumped into Des Barrit. He wished me well with Falstaff. I reminded him that when he did it, in Mike Attenborough's 2000 production, I'd never seen the plays in performance before, and so I had a sense of discovering Falstaff for the first time, and it was like finding a new statue by Michelangelo or concerto by Mozart. Here was a great, great creation by Shakespeare, unknown to me. It made me weep – in wonder at the writer's genius, and in joy at Des's playing. I've always relished his comic style – that big, comfortable, almost lazy presence – I'd seen him use it to tremendous effect as Bottom and Malvolio, and now as Falstaff.

However much I'm currently trying to deny the funny side of Falstaff, it's irresistible when an actor like Des makes it work.

Friday 18 October

Well, the *Richard II* reviews are terrific – five and four stars everywhere – and Greg could not have begun his leadership in any better way.

Before last night's show, we had dinner in the theatre's Rooftop Restaurant, and one of our guests was Thelma (Holt; producer and friend). I half-heard her and Greg discussing *Death of Salesman*. The RSC has been trying to get the rights for a couple of years now – for me to play Willy Loman – and Thelma has been acting as broker between us and the Miller Estate. So far no luck. Greg wants to schedule it for 2015, the centenary of Miller's birth, but others must have noticed this anniversary too, and our fear is that some big star

Des Barrit as Falstaff

has snatched it up. Anyway, Thelma was part of a conference call with the Estate today.

This afternoon she rang us in great excitement. We've got it! I'm doing it!

Good God. Falstaff and then Willy Loman.

Monday 21 October

Greg's down in London, and it's a filthy day here – dark and wet – but no Monday-morning low. Propped my script in its new position – on the table with the river view – and spent three hours revising *Part I*, most of which I know (big speeches only). In just six weeks, that's not bad going.

Managed to get hold of Stephen Fry's email address, and sent him our thanks and praise for his TV documentary *Out There*. This looked at gay life in homophobic countries, like Uganda and Russia. The really extreme places, like Iran, wouldn't allow him to film, so you just glimpsed footage of gay young men being hanged. Sequences like this, and the interviews that Stephen did with several rabid homophobes, upset me deeply. In the relatively short period of my own life, gay rights has made extraordinary progress: when I arrived in England in 1968 it was only one year after the Wolfenden Report and the legalisation of homosexuality, and yet fast-forward just thirty-seven years to 2005, and I was able to have a civil partnership with Greg. I could be forgiven for believing that the world had become a decent and fair place. Not so. Only part of the world. Stephen's programme showed the rest of it.

Tuesday 22 October

Another three-hour session this morning. I've moved into *Part II*. So all the pleasure of deciphering the lines again, all that delightful, clerical cross-checking to be done. When the notes in the RSC and Arden editions don't provide what I need, I have another source, a special helpline:

On the phone to Greg at lunchtime, I said, 'In Falstaff's first scene, he talks of "that foolish compounded clay, man". Explain please.'

'Think of "Man" with a capital "M", Mankind, and Adam was formed of earth, or clay, so it's just "foolish Mankind".'

By chance, Greg was being interviewed today about the new film of *Romeo and Juliet*. The screenwriter, Julian Fellowes, has simplified the text, saying that you need a university degree to understand Shakespeare. Bollocks. I'm a dumb South African *outjie*, who was taught Shakespeare very poorly at school, and never went to university. Yet by the time I put Falstaff in front of an audience, I will convey a *sense* of the meaning of every single line. The trouble with filming Shakespeare, is that they don't rehearse enough, if at all. The *Romeo and Juliet* cast would never have done the work I'm doing at the moment.

It's not a university degree you need for Shakespeare, but the craft and graft of classical acting.

Sunday 27 October

There's news of a Great Storm headed towards the UK, a hurricane on a scale we haven't known before. It's being nicknamed St Jude.

We've made some preparations. Did a big shop at Waitrose, filled the fridge, moved the furniture on our little patio against the wall, upturning the table.

In the past, when the Avon has flooded, it has never spilled onto this (the higher) bank, but what if St Jude breaks the rules? I find myself glancing round our small, overfilled flat: the floors are piled with Greg's papers and files, my sketchbooks and scripts, our photo albums. What would we save in an emergency?

As there are more and more warnings about travel disruptions, Greg cancels his trip to London tomorrow for auditions.

This is a strange feeling. A strange kind of apprehension. People must know it in other parts of the world, but not here.

Throughout the evening, we find ourselves *listening*. For the wind to grow. For Nature to do something.

But nothing.

As we go to bed, I write on my notepad: Am I hearing, actually hearing, the calm before the storm?

Monday 28 October

Well, it seems to have passed us by completely. We turned on BBC Breakfast News, and indeed there were catastrophic scenes along the south coast, and even parts of London, but it moved across the country without coming our way, and is now headed across the North Sea.

The morning here was beautiful, full of sunshine: the sky very blue, the grass very green, and the Avon that muddy brown, the colour of oxtail soup, which always reminds me of rivers in country towns in South Africa.

Greg suddenly had the day off, so we cleared a couple of tables, and spread out some special manuscripts.

Greg had commissioned a student at the Shakespeare Institute to collate all the cuts from previous RSC productions of the *Henries*, using the stage-management prompt copies which are stored at the Birthplace Trust in Henley Street. This student has now provided us with a stack of scripts (*Parts I* and *II*), each with the full text, the cuts marked in red, also running times and other details, recording what edited versions of the plays were presented in 1964 (directed by Peter Hall and John Barton), 1976 (Terry Hands), 1991 (Adrian Noble), 2000 (Mike Attenborough), 2007 (Mike Boyd).

So today we compared and contrasted these with our own cut copy. It was like being surrounded by a group of wise counsellors; as if those directors were in the room themselves, but without their egos – *oich*, imagine the scene in reality! – no, just in benign and generous mood, just there to help us. It was useful that we knew them all personally, knew their tastes, and had our own attitudes to them: 'So what did Terry do here?… and Adrian?… and the Great Barton?' Some of their cuts coincided with our own, some were startlingly more drastic, some we rejected outright, some were inspiring, and some weren't cuts, but *additions* – from the Quarto. These were mostly irresistible:

In Falstaff's first scene with the Lord Chief Justice, he has a speech where he complains about being sent to war again. The new line allows him to say, 'It was always yet the trick of our English nation, if they have a good thing to make it too common.' Which roughly translates as, 'Just because I'm the hero of Shrewsbury, I'm now our country's secret weapon!'

And in the Gloucestershire scene, when Falstaff is gossiping about Shallow, scandalously, there's a new line, which claims that he was 'lecherous as a monkey, and the whores called him Mandrake.' Delightful.

In the past a director, if so inclined, could visit the Birthplace Trust, and, under supervision, examine the prompt scripts of his predecessors. But Greg wants to get them reproduced like these today (maybe online), and made available to each new director, should they want them.

It's a wonderful archive that the RSC holds. What other theatre company could offer such guidance, such riches, for the preparation of a Shakespeare production?

The hours flew by. With us, alongside the Avon, working on Shakespeare. A perfect Stratford day.

Saturday 2 November

London.

We've come down for a big event at the National: the celebration of their fiftieth anniversary. There's a gala in the Olivier, which is being broadcast live on BBC2.

Before the show began, Nick Hytner came on stage, to explain the proceedings: 'This evening fulfils one of my secret desires – to tell an audience how to behave.'

There followed a series of extracts from the National's hits, some performed onstage, some filmed. One of the most moving was Joan Plowright doing a speech from *Saint Joan* (filmed a few days earlier on the stage of the Old Vic), still with the same good, down-to-earth honesty that she was blessed with as a young actress.

For me, other highlights were: film of Scofield in *Amadeus* (Christ, the power of the man!), Judi Dench live, doing one of Cleopatra's speeches, a sequence from *War Horse*, another from *Jerry Springer*, and a scene from *Angels in America*.

The show overran (I wonder what they did on BBC2?), and it was going on for midnight when it finished. So we found Nick, congratulated him, and slipped away.

It's funny – although I've had two big successes at the National (Pam Gems's *Stanley* and my own *Primo*), it's never felt like home, in the way that the RSC does.

Thursday 7 November

Stratford.

With the sun shining on the river, I had the surprising experience of learning Falstaff's last scene: the rejection by Hal. It's very moving. How does Shakespeare do it? How does he make us care so much for this cowardly, criminal old bullshitter? Don't know. It's a wonder. Literally. Just like there are wonders of Nature, there are wonders of Art, and the creation of Falstaff is one of them.

For the record, I began learning this role on the 10th of September and today is the 7th of November. About two months, working between two and three hours on weekday mornings. I've only learned the main speeches, so it's only about half the part, and it's not properly inside me yet – I could no sooner stand up and do it without the script than fly – but it's roughed in. And I've still got a month and a half before rehearsals…

Tuesday 12 November

When the autumn weather allows, we begin each day with a river walk. I find these as refreshing as dipping in the sea; it's the same kind of tonic, setting you up for the day's work. We either go out of town, alongside the fields, or – as today – cross the footbridge and traverse the other bank, before looping back.

As the path turned the corner at the Witter Lock, and we were presented with that sudden view of Holy Trinity Church, we both stopped in our tracks, and one, or both of us, said, 'Just look at that!' The church is already a remarkable place, housing as it does a remarkable grave, but to see it from this side of the Avon, with it on the higher bank, and the graveyard lifting it even higher, like a great work of art on a giant pedestal, and to see it on a bright blue morning, with the gorgeous gold, red and rust colours of the surrounding trees, and these reflected again in the still river, and this with a slight mist on it – oh, it was a marvellous thing.

Meanwhile, our talk was of casting. Hotspur. The only main role still free. So important. And so hard to find the right actor. Made harder by the fact that Hal is being played by Alex Hassell. He's such a dynamic stage presence that he could trespass into Hotspur's territory. The challenge is to find someone who has even more fire, more danger. Greg has three ideas for it, but his favourite is Trevor White, the Canadian actor who played Aufidius in his production of *Coriolanus*. He was terrific. I'd be very happy if he did Hotspur.

Friday 15 November

Back in March, I did a drawing of myself trying to decide whether to do Falstaff. Today I had my first go at drawing myself in the role. I've no idea what the actual 'look' will be, or the costume, or anything, so this was just an impression, just how the character feels at this point in time.

Working from some of the photos that Stewart Hemley took of me at Hampstead last month, I sketched in a very free way, letting the crayon marks go all over the place, wild and wavy for the hair and beard, patchy and criss-crossed for the booze-blasted face, and then blurring them, smearing them. I stopped well short of a homage to Francis Bacon, but I had him in mind. He'd have done a good portrait of Falstaff; he *was* Falstaff!

The end result bore only a vague resemblance to me, but, more importantly, did it look like Falstaff?

I'd say... *ish*. Something too benign about him, too polite. As though he's posed for the drawing in a rather well-mannered way. There needs to be a darker edge to him.

That's fine. That's helpful, in fact. The part is unformed at this point in time. This shows the way forward...

Saturday 16 November

Back from London, Greg liked the drawing, and said it made him excited about doing the show.

'How would you describe his expression?' I asked.

'Oh, like someone has just given him a cup of sack and some nice cheese.'

This confirmed my reservations. Falstaff's appetite is for more than sack and cheese. They're only fuel. He actually wants to consume all the rules and regulations in the world, all the order of the universe.

1st sketch of me as Falstaff

Tuesday 19 November

On this morning's river walk, when we crossed the Tramway foot-bridge just past the theatre, we didn't loop back to Avonside, but went on to the far end of town, where our new house is situated, the Artistic Director's house. In fact, we lived in it before – when Adrian Noble had The Job, he bought a house outside Stratford – but the renovation is so extensive it's like a different place. The builder, David Neale, showed us round. It's in a rough-and-ready state at the moment, but the potential is exciting. A much bigger kitchen, a guest suite above it, dormer windows in our bedroom and bathroom, which will flood those areas with light, and, best of all, my painting studio. It's considerably larger than it looked on the architect's plans, and will have French windows, with a splendid view of rolling fields. The best thing is that the floor is going to be made of some of the teak and mahogany stage-boards retrieved from the old theatre.

I'm a great believer in ghosts in the walls, of all theatres, and in their stages especially. Just think of the actors who have bestrode this one. I'm going to have Laurence Olivier under my feet...!

Monday 25 November

We spent the weekend in North Wales with Greg's family, celebrating his fifty-fifth birthday. Pleased to have bright weather for our drive back this morning. Coming into the Vale of Llangollen was a breathtaking moment: a giant bowl of sunlit mist with the flame of autumn trees showing through here and there.

We took a little detour to Shrewsbury, to visit the battlefield site there – the location for the climax of *Henry IV Part I*. Not much to see. The viewing mound overlooked a huge pylon and a path for dog walkers. Further on, the Church of Mary Magdalene (built to commemorate the victory) was closed. So our chief pleasure turned out to be a rather Falstaffian one: discovering the Battlefield 1403 Farm Shop, which was filled with goodies, from big home-cooked meat pies to little bottles of damson gin. We stocked up greedily.

Tuesday 26 November

One of the lasting memories of my first experience of living in Stratford, during my debut RSC season in 1982, when I had rooms in the old Avonside mansion, was the sound of bell-ringing practice coming from Trinity Church on Tuesday evenings. In the thirty-one years since, whenever I've been here, that sound makes me stop whatever I'm doing, and listen for a moment, smiling.

Tonight I experienced it at close quarters.

Greg and I have become patrons of the church, which is quite odd for a gay couple, one of whom is Jewish. Anyway, this allowed us the special privilege of attending tonight's session.

Climbing the tower wasn't easy: a steep twist of narrow stone stairs with only a thick red cord to cling on to. Finally we reached the chamber where the bell ropes hang. A group of about a dozen people were assembling. All volunteers, not just from Stratford, but surrounding towns and villages as well, and mostly in middle or old age.

Before they started, we were taken up another floor – via an even more precarious staircase – to see the bells themselves. Great big brass things, brownish grey, patterned with bird droppings. Some quite temperamental, we were told. If you don't control your rope carefully, they can break their wooden cradles, and run amok, or rather ring amok.

Back in the main chamber, it was time. The first group took hold of their ropes – along a padded length – and began a curious rhythm, pulling down, letting go, pulling again. The lady next to us explained that everyone was playing the same tune, but at different times, like singing a round.

I noticed that the ringers were sometimes exchanging comments. 'What are they saying?' I asked our guide.

'Well, there's only four commands really,' she replied; 'One to start, one to stop, and a couple in-between. Oh, and occasionally a few expletives deleted if someone gets the timing wrong.'

Looking round the circle of gentle, focused, grey-haired faces, I thought the expletives deleted probably weren't much stronger than, 'Oh, for goodness' sake…!'

Each group did about ten to fifteen minutes. In one of the breaks, we were invited to try. I was too timid, but Greg had a go, taking the opportunity to explain who we were: '…and Tony is about to play Falstaff, who gets to say the famous line, "We have heard the chimes at midnight".'

'Not round here you won't!' exclaimed one old chap. 'We've got to stop at nine, or they complain in Old Town.'

We said our thanks and left them to it. Walking back to Avonside, hearing the bells strike up again, the sound was more enchanting than ever, now that I had a picture of that little chamber in the tower, brightly lit and nicely warmed, with a gathering of devoted folk who journey there on Tuesday evenings, to practise a skill they've learned carefully and take great pride in; it's a picture of Middle England, a picture which reminds me why I love this country.

Wednesday 27 November

Revised all the lines that I've learned so far, in both parts. Thought how different the river view was, in front of me, from six weeks ago, when *Hysteria* finished and I moved up here. The autumn was beautiful then. Now the light is grey, the water dull, the trees quite bare, the remaining leaves a flat yellow tone.

Thursday 28 November

With my script back on the drawing board in my London studio, I begin work on what I call the little lines: the quick-fire banter and exchanges with other characters. These are much harder than the big speeches to learn before rehearsals, without knowing the rhythm of your fellow actors, the interplay with them, and indeed the physical shape of the scene. Certain lines will become easy to remember when they're connected to a specific movement: *I'm sitting down at this point* or *I'm moving from A to B*. In the absence of these aids, the public's favourite question – 'How do you learn all those lines?' – is difficult to answer again. (Someone should do a study.) Today I find myself using all sorts of devices: word association, letter association, all kinds of alliteration, half-hidden tunes in the dialogue (Shakespeare is good with these), and other tricks. But why do some sections go into the brain quicker than others? And why do I stumble on a particular word or phrase again and again? These are easily solved – I write them out on a sheet of paper next to the script, and practise them more than the rest – but why do they happen in the first place? And as to the use of 'thee' or 'you', that's simply a bloody nightmare. There's not always an apparent logic, and sometimes they'll both appear in the same sentence. Then the task is simply one of repetition, of developing a kind of muscle memory with the line, like a dance step or a fight move: *it can only be this way.*

Friday 29 November

Stephen Brimson Lewis and Greg had a design meeting at the house today, upstairs in Greg's study. I only popped in at the end. Stephen had some images on his laptop of overweight chaps. 'You can google "Fat Men",' he said with an air of apology. 'Now, is it this, or this?' he asked, showing a fat man and an obese one. I chose the first, reiterating that it must be realistic, it has to be feasibly *me*. We agreed to meet the fat-suit maker soon, try out some shapes, and get a rehearsal version made.

In line-learning, one leapt out at me. *Part I*, Act Three, Scene Three. Mistress Quickly is telling Hal that Falstaff claims the prince owes him a thousand pounds. Hal confronts Falstaff. Falstaff replies, 'A thousand pound, Hal? A million. Thy love is worth a million. Thou ow'st me thy love.' Quick as a flash, Falstaff gets himself out of a tight corner, and gives a tender description of their friendship. Fine writing.

Stephen B.L. googling

Sunday 1 December

My God, we're in December. Rehearsals start this month...!

Thursday 5 December

To the Duchess Theatre, to see *Arturo Ui*. I have a complicated relationship with this play. Shortly after arriving in this country, I saw Leonard Rossiter play it in Michael Blakemore's production, and it remains one of the best pieces of character acting – no, of *acting* – I have ever seen: a walking cartoon, hilarious and chilling. When I came to play the part myself, at the National in 1990, I felt thwarted by the Brecht Estate forbidding us to use the George Tabori version (which Blakemore and Rossiter used): Tabori's version improves on Brecht's own work. At the time, I felt that this accounted for the disappointing time I had on that show. But, puzzlingly, the Brecht Estate have allowed this current production, from Chichester, to use the Tabori, and yet for me the play still falls flat. But it certainly works as a star vehicle, and Henry Goodman certainly delivered. He began in very grotesque form: a strange, shuffling, hunched figure, who gradually grew more upright, more presentable, more Hitlerian. It was mesmeric.

Afterwards, we were on our way backstage, to visit Henry, when Greg turned on his phone.

'Mandela has died,' he said.

I stopped in my tracks. It was expected, of course, but still a shock. We hailed the first taxi we saw, and Greg texted Henry to explain.

Back at home, we watched BBC News for a couple of hours. Although Obama, or his speech-writers, came up with a good sound bite – 'He no longer belongs to us, he belongs to the ages' – the President was clearly speaking from his own heart when he said that, if it wasn't for the inspiration he got from Mandela, he wouldn't be where he is today.

At one point, they showed Table Mountain and played 'Nkosi Sikelel''. We were both in tears. Greg said, 'Thank you for letting me know that country and meet that man.'

(Although I had met him before, Greg and I met him together in 2002, when we organised a gala at the Royal Festival Hall for the *Celebrate South Africa* festivities. Greg often talks about *the handshake*, which others have also described: how Mandela used his free hand to enfold their gripped hands, while meeting Greg's gaze with a deep, calm smile.)

Friday 6 December

The feeling is strange. It's as though I've lost someone close to me. But that's true in a way. He was close to us all, to the spirit of humanity. No, that's not true. Humanity is a pretty ugly thing – not like him at all. We marvel at him, we praise him, but we don't really recognise him. He's the kind of human being that religion pictures. He may have lived, but he's almost like a fantasy.

The *Guardian* was transformed. The front page was just one big photo of him.

On the *Today* programme, John Humphrys did a moving tribute, which included an interview from 1994, with a black woman who was queuing to vote in the first democratic elections; she was pregnant, and talked about how her child would know a different South Africa. There was also an interview with Denis Goldberg, the only white man among the accused at the Rivonia Trial. He reminded us that they were all expecting the death penalty. Just think.

Couldn't work today, couldn't do lines. Went into town, to buy some things for Christmas – which we'll be spending in South Africa.

Back at home, Rosinda (our cleaning lady) was ironing shirts downstairs. She's Portuguese, and isn't always fluent in English, yet said, 'A great star in the sky has gone out.'

Phoned home. Spoke to Verne (my sister) first. She said the good thing was that South Africa was united again, in a way it hasn't been for a long time: 'Black and white people are singing and dancing in the streets.'

Then spoke to Randall (my elder brother), who said, 'It's a day of great sadness for me. Y'know, if it wasn't for him, we might not be here any more.' He meant the whites. Although Mandela hadn't been in power for years, he was a controlling influence. Randall talked of his fear that South Africa could go the way of Zimbabwe. Mentioned the extremist, Julius Malema: 'He's not just the mad clown that people say… he's a clever politician… he's formed his own party, and he's very popular… among all the young people who have nothing, and nothing to lose.'

Jesus.

All my life, my family has been talking like this. Even under Apartheid, during the safest, sunniest days on those all-white beaches, when my people lazed in luxury, and my dad was Master Mannie, *die ou Baas*, even then he was forever trying to think of ways of getting money out of the country, 'a nest egg', just in case we ever had to flee, like his parents had from Lithuania. Then, as Apartheid was ending, the Shers were absolutely sure there'd be a catastrophic bloodbath. (To be fair, everyone thought the same, blacks and whites – the Miracle of Madiba had yet to happen.) And now it could all start up again…

Jesus.

Tuesday 10 December

While Greg went to his preview of *Richard II* – now transferred to the Barbican – I watched Mandela's Memorial Service on TV. Attended by Presidents, Prime Ministers, and thousands of spectators. Though not as many as expected: the vast stadium was only two-thirds full. Maybe because of the torrential rain. Which is a good sign in African culture; one man said, 'The gates of heaven

have opened for Nelson Mandela.' The biggest ovation was for
Obama, and the worst booing for Zuma – which must have been
quite a humiliation on this world stage. But it delighted his oppo-
nents. The ANC veteran Ronnie Kasrils was grinning as he said,
'The populace has spoken – it is truly Shakespearean!'

Wednesday 11 December

Blush, the beloved country.

Three disgraceful things have emerged about yesterday's Memorial for Mandela:

The SABC (South African Broadcasting Corporation) didn't show
the booing of Zuma. The organisation is censoring the news just like
they did when they served the Apartheid government.

The man who was signing for the deaf, standing alongside each
speaker, was a fake: he was signing gibberish. He's been identified as
mentally ill, with a tendency to violence. Obama's team must be flab-
bergasted that the South Africans saw fit to put this man right next
to their President.

Worst of all, somehow. Knowing that Desmond Tutu was at the
service, thieves broke into his Cape Town home, and burgled it. It's
happened several times before, apparently: once they even stole his
Nobel Prize.

Each of these things – the corruption, the incompetence, the
crime – are so typically South African. I don't say that with any ease.

Thursday 12 December

Richard II's London press night. This was a significant moment: the
RSC back at the Barbican. I'm delighted about it. There was
something terribly self-destructive about our quitting the place in
2002 before we'd found an alternative base. We simply became one
of the homeless in London. We drifted around, trying the West End,
the Roundhouse, and a couple of other venues, but we were no
longer a significant presence in the capital city. So – we must thank
the Barbican for welcoming us in again. But it did feel strange
arriving there tonight, particularly as the first thing I saw was a giant
picture of me – the ad for the *Henries*, which will play here next
autumn. Otherwise, it was all as I remembered: the foyers as hopeless

as before, with acres of deserted space, and the auditorium as splendid. The production sat beautifully on the stage, and the cast rose to the occasion. David Tennant was even better than in Stratford. As his world collapsed around him, he tried behaving as he always had – preening, not caring – but you knew what he was feeling. It was very moving. As was the standing ovation at the end.

My boy did well.

Friday 13 December

The Story of Falstaff's Ring.

During this morning's line-learning I got sidetracked and ended up piecing together a picture of Falstaff's life.

It began when I became intrigued by a line in *Part I*, Act Three, Scene Three. Falstaff is complaining to Mistress Quickly about having his pockets picked in the tavern, and says, 'I have lost a seal ring of my grandfather's worth forty mark.' (A mark was two-thirds of a pound at that time, so a considerable amount of money.) Quickly claims she's heard Hal say it was a cheap copper ring. And indeed when Hal now enters, he calls the ring 'a trifle, some eight-penny matter.' So which version is true? Maybe both. Maybe Falstaff did possess a valued family heirloom, but maybe it was used in some shady deal or lost one drunken night, and maybe in recent years he's been wearing a worthless replacement.

It set me thinking about Falstaff's history. He's so much a creature of the present, he so fully occupies the space before your eyes, the here and now, that you don't stop to think about him existing in any other time frame. Yet there's another tantalising line in his last speech in *Part I* (Act Five, Scene Three): 'If I do grow great again...' *Again?* I suggested cutting this word, but Greg wanted to leave it in, hinting at some former, more elevated way of life. A life where people had seal rings worth forty mark.

In *Part II* there is more detail about Falstaff's family. In Act Two, Scene Two, Poins reads a letter from Falstaff, in which he refers to 'my brothers and sister'. Dear God, there are more of them. A family of Falstaffs. What does the sister look like?!

And Justice Shallow is full of information about him in Act Three, Scene Two. Recalling his own young adulthood, Shallow says, 'Then was Jack Falstaff, now Sir John, a boy, and page to Thomas Mowbray,

Duke of Norfolk.' (Pages were often from top families, put into service to learn about life at court.) Shallow also reports that Falstaff beat up the King's jester Scoggin, fought well with a backsword, and, when he was older, joined Shallow in what sounds like a threesome with the salaciously named Jane Nightwork. But is Shallow's word reliable? Well, later in the same scene, Falstaff himself remembers being with Shallow at Clement's Inn (one of the Inns of Chancery) and the lewd goings-on there.

So – fragments of the Fat Knight's biography.

None of which an actor can actually play.

Other than to give him a certain inbred grandness.

Not in his *look* – I feel sure of that; he's fallen on hard times, he's become a thief – but maybe in his *sound*.

I try a few lines in an old-fashioned, plummy accent; the kind that has a laziness to it, dragging two vowels into one – 'cowards' becomes 'cow'ds' (almost 'cards') – and a satirical tone, which clamps quotation marks around every other word or phrase. So, for example, entering the tavern scene, he says:

'A plague of all cow'ds, I say... is there no "virtue extant"?'

Yes, sounds good, sounds right.

And it coincides with something Greg said to me some time ago, 'His voice is going to be much posher than yours, isn't it?'

Sunday 15 December

In the days when I was seriously doubting whether I could play Falstaff, I'm glad I didn't see Bernard Shaw's review of Beerbohm Tree's performance in 1896:

'Mr Tree only wants one thing to make him an excellent Falstaff, and that is to get born over again, as unlike himself as possible.'

Tuesday 17 December

Greg was on the phone to his sister, Jo. I heard him say, 'We start Monday week.' (Meaning rehearsals.) I thought he'd made a mistake, then realised he hadn't. It's incredible to think we're going all the way to South Africa and back *before* Monday week. Even more incredibly, on Monday week, Falstaff will cease to be a mass of lines that I'm learning, and will become my new role, my new job.

Wednesday 25 December

Cape Town, South Africa. Christmas Day.

We're staying at The Mount Nelson (the grand old hotel from colonial times), in one of the garden cottages at the back, alongside a smaller, quieter swimming pool than the main one. Kids and mobile phones are banned here – oh joy.

Our cottage has a lovely *stoep* (porch) and this is where we sit this morning, before going to the big family lunch. Greg has his head buried in his book, *The Fears of Henry IV*, by Ian Mortimer (who'll be visiting rehearsals), but I find it difficult to read anything, do anything, other than soak in the sensations of my childhood. The particular blueness of the sky and brightness of the light. The birds: the glorious, noisy ha-di-dahs (ibises), the glossy starlings with that brown flash on their wings, the Cape doves doing their distinctive call. The insects: big, African-sized orange-and-white butterflies fluttering over our garden of roses and busy Lizzies, and brown-and-blue dragonflies darting round the pool. On the far side, two more sights which fill me with nostalgia: a hedge of pink hydrangeas (like the ones Mom used to cultivate at home), and the tawny flanks of Signal Hill, from where, every day at noon, you hear the thud of the cannon which is fired up there.

At 12.45, Verne and Joan (her partner) collect us at the front of the hotel, and drive us up to the suburb called Highlands Estate, where Heidi and Ed (Randall's middle daughter and her husband) are renting a house. It's right next to Table Mountain. When I get out of the car, I sway back on my feet, astonished to find myself so close to this famous rock. All week the South-Easter has been blowing, which creates, along the top, a low, rolling cloud – the so-called tablecloth – but today the weather is still, and the sunlight on the stone has an extraordinary quality. I like to think that it comes from the fact that the mountain stands on the very end of Africa, above the freezing Atlantic, with the next land mass being the Antarctic. So even on a baking hot day like this, there's an icy clarity to the light, almost like the light on a glacier.

There are twenty-four of us assembled for lunch. Greg is proud of the fact that a few years ago he introduced Christmas to my Jewish family, who had never celebrated it before, and are now hooked.

Someone announces: 'Presents, presents – gather all kids and Christians!'

Originally, Greg was the only Christian, and the only adult to get presents, but the family has acquired a few more since.

When it comes to the meal, different households provide the different courses. Our contribution is a huge Christmas pudding from Fortnum and Mason: their King George plum special. Normally I have to watch my weight carefully on holiday, but not this time; I have a special dispensation, called the Falstaff licence, and can pig myself silly. The lunch is taken slowly, with long breaks, when people go outside to sunbathe or swim in the pool. Not very Christmassy, but very South African.

At the end, champagne is poured and Randall stands to make the toast. Trying to get silence, he quotes Tutu from Mandela's Memorial the other day: 'Not until I hear a pin drop!' Randall is a natural public speaker, and on good form today. He pays credit to those among us who've made big changes in their lives during the last year – including Greg running the RSC.

In reply, Greg tells the assembled that he's got conclusive proof of why he has a rightful place among the Shers, and holds aloft a book we found at Exclusive Books on the Waterfront. Called *The Historical Karoo* (the vast area of semi-desert north of Cape Town) by Chris Schoeman.

'…It's got a chapter on Middlepost!' Greg says.

'*Oich*, Middlepost,' says Yvette (Randall's wife); 'The one-horse town where the horse died.'

Greg explains that the author mentions my novel *Middlepost*, and how it's a fictional account of how my grandfather came to own the tiny *dorp*, building a motel, shop, and petrol station, and running it as a stopping-off place for long-distance commercial travellers (South Africa's Willy Lomans). The chapter also describes the Battle of Middlepost during the Boer War, when General Jan Smuts led a Boer Commando against the British troops at the settlement. The account of the battle is given by no less a figure than Arthur Conan Doyle, who, having created Sherlock Holmes and killed him off, was serving as a medical orderly during the war. He recounts how, when the Brits were losing, the cavalry rode in to the rescue, led by a young captain by the name of Doran…!

Everyone is suitably impressed by the coincidence, and cheers. Greg doesn't go on to say that Captain Doran failed to save the situation, and the Boers won. To this day there's a gravestone at Middlepost – I remember it from childhood holidays – honouring the soldiers of the Imperial Yeomanry who were killed there.

When we read this section in the book the other day, Greg said, 'So in this one little snapshot, you get General Smuts, Sherlock Holmes, Grandfather Sher and Captain Doran!'

'I must tell Terry Johnson,' I said; 'There's a play in it.'

Friday 27 December

Managed to squeeze in lunch with our closest friends here: Janice (Honeyman; theatre director – she did the *Tempest* that I was in) and Liza (Key; documentary film-maker). A visit to Cape Town would be incomplete without seeing them. Janice spoke eloquently about Mandela's death: 'You see, the Miracle of Madiba is that over and over again he brings out a togetherness, a unity between people here. And it's absolutely heartfelt. The ecstasy we felt when he gave us the possibility of salvation in 1994… it was kind of repeated when he died. As we were celebrating his life, there was an amazing closeness between everyone, a euphoria. There are times when this place can seem to be disintegrating, morally, but maybe his death has given us another chance to pull together, to hold together.'

I sat hushed, wishing I shared her optimism. But they live here – they know better.

In my preparations for Falstaff, I've been too squeamish to watch programmes like *Embarrassing Bodies*, to study obesity, but this afternoon a man elected to give me a full-frontal, real-life display of the condition.

We were at the poolside, and I swear we heard him coming before we saw him: a small rumble in the earth like the arrival of Tyrannosaurus Rex in *Jurassic Park*. Then he loomed into view, wearing nothing but sunglasses and swimming trunks, all the rest of his mountainous flesh on display. Of course I've seen severely overweight people before, but never as naked as this. He carried a walking stick; didn't use it, but held it like a weapon. This added to the sense of danger that he somehow possessed; if he was prepared to commit this amount of self-harm, what might he do to others?

'But Falstaff can't be like that,' Greg whispeared; 'We can't fear for his health.'

'No, no,' I answered; 'And we've agreed – he's not going to be this size. But all the same…!'

The best thing was that he stared at *us* with incredulity: these two mature chaps with no females in sight. Greg and I don't kiss and cuddle in public, but there's an intimacy between us – looks and smiles, handing one another towels and sun oil – that belie our being just friends. This man certainly spotted it straight away.

Good for you, I thought – yes, let human beings gawp at one another in disbelief.

Back on the *stoep* of our cottage, I did some discreet drawings of him. I plan to work them up into a picture called *Falstaff at the Pool*.

Tonight we go to the part of Cape Town that I know best, the area where I grew up, at the far end of Sea Point, just before it turns into Bantry Bay. This time of year would have been the long summer holidays in my schooldays, so every sensation touches me in a tender way – it's from my youth, it's in my blood – and all so different from the life I've led ever since in England. On summertime evenings in the Northern Hemisphere, it's the light that lingers. Here the sun sets fast, the night is immediately dark, and it's the heat of the day that lingers; it's very sensual – as is the smell and sound of the sea… this is always present, the sea…

We're having a *braai* (barbecue) at Montagu House, which used to be the Sher family home. After Mom's death in 2006, it was left to us four children. Joel (my younger brother) bought up our shares, and created his own home here, with Eileen (wife) and Beth (daughter). Among the extensive renovations, he built a big brick *braai* on one of the decks – he's the best *braai*er in town – and this is where we gather for our farewell meal.

Farewell – already?

I knew it would hurt – the shortness of this holiday – and it does. And although I'm glad Joel has kept the house in the family, being here hurts a bit too. Nothing is recognisable – until I go to the loo, and notice the wrought-iron stair rail leading upstairs. That's exactly the same as in childhood. Except it seemed fancier then, and bigger…

As we're saying our goodbyes, everyone wishes us well for Monday.

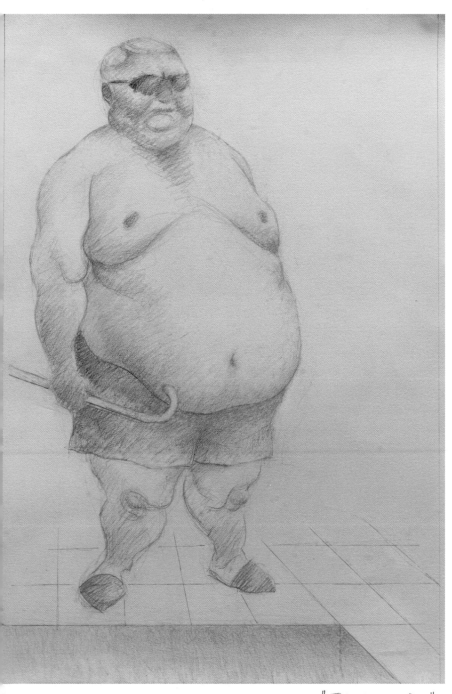

"Falstaff at the Pool"

'Why, what's happening then?' says Greg, making them laugh –
while a little flutter goes through my belly. It's going to be there, I
think, for many months to come.

4. Three Rehearsal Rooms

Monday 30 December

London.

The British winter always comes as a shock after our Christmas holidays in South Africa. Not the cold, the rain, or snow, but the lack of light. These bad-light days: blighty days, as I call them.

Anyway, no Monday-morning gloom today, for today we start the biggest venture of our working life together. All sorts of feelings are prickling away inside me, excitement and fear, but certainly no gloom.

Before we leave the house, we do the ritual that launches all our projects. On the mantelpiece of our dining-room fireplace stands a wooden carving which we bought in India some years ago. It's of Ganesh, the Hindu god of Good Beginnings and Obstacles, which is an appropriate title for any rehearsal period. We take a pinch of red kumkuma powder from a container, and throw it onto the elephant-headed figure, making a wish. Your wish can't be for yourself, but in this case our wishes are virtually interchangeable: mine is for his production, and I presume his is for my performance.

Clapham High Street is a long stretch of mini-supermarkets, hardware shops and scruffy cafés; it's not my favourite place, particularly on a grey day, but this is where the RSC rehearsal rooms are situated: a characterless building with a big open space on each floor. We're on the top.

God, the shows I've done here, I think as I climb the stairs, but the memories – all good, as it happens – provide no protection against the first-day-at-school nerviness that accompanies me into the room. It's ridiculous. I've been an actor for over forty years, yet I'm as anxious today as I was when I started out.

The room is long and high, and large enough to have the footprint of the main Stratford stage marked out on the floor. The tall windows overlook the surrounding buildings, and have black drapes, which have to be drawn when the low December sun slants in, making you shade your eyes. We're moving to a different location in a few weeks, so this is rehearsal room number one.

Actors are arriving, pulling off overcoats, scarves and hats. Most of the cast are strangers to me. I say hello to Alex Hassell (playing Hal): he's got a big open smile, and looks great – tanned from a trip to India. Then I make a beeline for someone I know very well indeed: Jim (Hooper, my former partner, now closest friend), who's playing Silence and Vernon. It's going to be a comfort having him as a travelling companion on the journey ahead.

When everyone's assembled, Greg does a brief talk, introducing some key RSC folk: Catherine Mallyon, Jeremy Adams (our producer), and John Wyver (who'll be in charge of our broadcast, Live-from-Stratford). Greg also explains why we're starting on this unlikely date: although we'll lose Wednesday (New Year's Day), it still gains us an extra week. We've got eleven in all, for two plays.

(I'm not convinced that's enough. Greg's argument is that although it's two plays it's only one character – which will speed things up.)

Now Greg says, 'We're going to do a little icebreaking game. Technical team and stage management are welcome to participate, but actors *have* to.'

As I watch all the non-actors flee for the exits, I think: *Games –* whether on sporting fields, at parties, or in rehearsals – *I hate them!*

This one involves us walking around the room, greeting one another, and imparting three facts about ourselves. Then we'll each sit in the hot seat, and the group will try to remember what they've learned about us.

As I stroll round, I tell people I was born in Cape Town, I have a wool allergy, and one other thing which is sure to 'break the ice'.

When we go into the next part of the game, the hot seat, I begin to see the point and pleasure of the exercise: we have, very quickly, got to know one another. Sometimes the facts are trivial – the names of pets or favourite colours – sometimes more important: someone was almost stolen as a baby, someone else fell out of a helicopter.

My turn comes. As soon as I sit in the hot seat, people start to shout out the third fact I told them:

'He's sleeping with the director!'

Greg gives a spluttering laugh: 'You told them that?'

'I did,' I reply; 'I thought it best they knew.'

Josh Richards (playing Bardolph and Glendower) pipes up: 'It's the only reason he got the part!'

'Absolutely true,' I say, and then to Greg: 'Now we're both blushing.'

Much laughter.

(Though there was a time when Josh would have been giving voice to my very real fear.)

Now Greg does a talk about the plays, and about Shakespeare. He's always felt that the RSC needs to help those young actors who are joining for the first time, and who may feel ignorant about our resident playwright. He claims it's how he felt when he arrived as an actor in '87, which I don't quite believe (he was living and breathing Shakespeare as a schoolboy), but it's certainly how I felt back in '82.

He's brought along some books in a canvas bag we got at Shrewsbury, with the logo *Battlefield 1403*, and lifts out his facsimile of the First Folio. 'Here's my favourite page,' he says, showing the group the list of actors in Shakespeare's company: Richard Burbage, Will Kemp (who probably played Falstaff) and the rest. Greg relates stories about many of them. We listen, enchanted – we, modern-day actors – basking in their long-ago glory.

'Thank God I don't have to read Falstaff today,' I said to Greg as we gathered round the table for this afternoon's session. He's the only director I know who doesn't do a read-through on the first day. Maybe because he was an actor, and knows how crucifying it can be. We all try to pretend it's not a kind of audition (even though you've already got the part), but judgements *are* made.

Nevertheless, we do start reading *Part I*. We go round the circle, each reading whichever part is next, as long as it's not our own – the rule is you can't read your own part – and then 'translating' the speeches into everyday English. We're aided by the notes in the various editions on the table: as well as the ones I've been using – the RSC and the Arden – there is the Oxford, the Pelican, the New Penguin, the New Cambridge, as well as an invaluable bible, the Crystals' *Shakespeare's Words:A Glossary and Language Companion*.

Some surprises as we proceed. In Act One, Scene Scene, Westmoreland tells of the fate of Mortimer's forces against Glendower; the butchery and mutilation of soldiers:

> Such beastly shameless transformation
> By those Welshwomen done as may not be
> Without much shame retold or spoken of.

We look at one another, frowning in puzzlement. Then Josh Richards, who's Welsh, says, 'I've known a few women like that back home.'

We laugh and are about to move on, when Simon Thorp (playing Blunt and Lord Chief Justice) looks up from his Arden edition, and says there's a note about the mutilations. They involved the cutting off of penises and sticking them in mouths, and the cutting off of noses and sticking them in anuses. Stunned, we turn back to Josh, who says:

'Oh yes, there was this lady in Cardiff…!'

Tuesday 31 December

Continued reading *Part I* round the table. How well British actors sight-read Shakespeare, how fluently. (While I struggle and stumble my way through whatever part I'm allotted.) But this same facility can be deceptive. Most Shakespeare productions don't go through the process we're doing at the moment, and the actors can end up speaking the text with lots of flair but little meaning. Greg's shows are praised for their clarity. Here's why. And it's important for the company to do this together, so that we all understand the whole play. It's particularly good for those actors playing small parts – they develop an investment in the work which they might not otherwise feel.

This afternoon we stopped paraphrasing (we'll come back to it) and just read the rest of *Part I*. Greg wants us to have read both parts by the end of the week.

Josh Richards with cup of tea

At the end of rehearsals, Greg suggested a New Year's toast. Stage management brought in several bottles of Pedro Ximénez, and trays of little plastic glasses. Spanish sherry is thought to be close to sack, the Elizabethan drink which is much referred to in the plays.

As we raise our glasses, Greg says, 'Here's to a happy new year!' Laughing, he adds, 'At least I hope so, since we'll be spending most of it together.'

We drink, and pull our faces. It's sweet and syrupy. It would be impossible to have it in the vast quantities that Falstaff and his cronies consume. So sack must be something different. I volunteer to make it my research project. (Others are doing the Crusades, the Battle of Shrewsbury, etc.)

It's liberating to no longer go to New Year's Eve parties – like Richard Wilson's legendary Hogmanay bashes in the eighties and nineties – to no longer stay up late for them, work out how to get there and back, and also, in my case, coke-sniff my way through the jollities, and begin every new year completely wrecked.

These days we go to bed at ten, and simply miss all the fuss.

It's very liberating.

Wednesday 1 January 2014

'Happy New Year,' we murmured on waking. Greg said he heard the fireworks on the Thames at midnight ('the chimes at midnight'), but I slept straight through.

How strange and wonderful to have a day off *already*.

We made a roast chicken lunch, and for dessert tried the Pedro Ximénez sherry poured over vanilla ice cream – as recommended on the bottle. Absolutely delicious.

The weather was miserable – grey and rainy – but perfect for an afternoon movie on the telly. It was *The Sound of Music*. We were both pushovers for it; Greg said, 'It's the sound of childhood.' Mind you, he was six when it came out (1965), and I was sixteen.

Thursday 2 January

Back at work. This week is quite confusing.

Oliver Ford Davies (playing Shallow) joined rehearsals. I'm a big fan of his. Not only is he a very fine actor, but a very bright mind.

We launched into *Part II*. There's a lot of sickness in the story now: the King is sick, Northumberland is sick (or feigning sickness), Falstaff talks of deafness, gout and pox, and says that even his purse suffers from consumption, Doll Tearsheet has the clap... the whole country is ill. Shakespeare weaves this thread throughout the play, without drawing attention to it, and subtly creates a completely different atmosphere to *Part I*. That's good writing.

I was particularly interested in 'the other scenes' (those without Falstaff), and much struck by King Henry's speech about insomnia in Act Three, Scene One. Shakespeare is obsessed by sleep, as in *Macbeth* ('the death of each day's life, sore labour's bath, / Balm of hurt minds, great nature's second course...'). I was talking to Jasper Britton (playing the King) afterwards, saying how the sleep speech surprised me. Overhearing, Greg said, 'It's only because you never read the parts of the play you're not in!'

'Correct,' I said, braving it out; 'I'm taking a Mike Leigh approach to this, where you only know what your character knows, only his world, and not the rest of the story.'

I'm still planning to play Falstaff as an alcoholic; I mean, explicitly. Am reading a book called *The Trip to Echo Spring* by Olivia Laing, which is about famous writers with drink problems, and find myself wondering whether Falstaff's situation is like these men, where booze is such an integral part of their society that all boundaries get blurred. When Scott Fitzgerald's health is deteriorating, he tries to stop drinking, but that only means 'hard liquor' (spirits) – he still drinks massive quantities of beer. Meanwhile, Ernest Hemingway is contemptuous of his buddy Fitzgerald starting to behave like a drunkard. Hemingway boasts of being able to 'drink hells any amount of whisky without getting drunk'. That could be Falstaff talking. Hemingway also says, 'I have drunk since I was fifteen and few things have given me more pleasure... Modern life is often a mechanical oppression and liquor is the only mechanical relief.' Is there something of Hemingway in Falstaff? The ultimate swaggerer, yet also gifted. Falstaff has such a glorious, disrespectful, unique view of the world, that maybe in another life he could've been a great artist or writer...

Saturday 4 January

Stratford-upon-Avon.

...Talking of great writers, I met Hilary Mantel today. We've come up to see her double bill (adapted for the stage by Mike Poulton): *Wolf Hall* and *Bring Up the Bodies*. Apparently, she so enjoyed this theatrical outing of her work she said it was better than winning the Booker twice. She was perfectly charming, but didn't really want to sit and have a drink with us, preferring to walk round the foyers: 'People will recognise me, and then we can talk about it all!'

The shows were excellent, staged with simplicity and fluidity by Jeremy Herrin, the text sparkling with wit (don't know if that's Mantel or Poulton; probably both), and a very strong cast, particularly Ben Miles, Nathaniel Parker, Paul Jesson, and Lucy Briers.

Press day is Wednesday. It doesn't really matter what the critics say – the entire run sold out before it opened – but if it is well received this could be another real humdinger hit for the RSC. Following *Richard II* and *Wendy and Peter Pan*, it's getting Greg's reign off to a tremendous start.

'Let's hope the *Henries* don't let the side down,' I said to Greg. We both laughed nervously.

Sunday 5 January

There's been wild weather around the country: coastal storms and inland flooding.

Overnight the Avon has swollen enormously and flooded – just the opposite bank again, mercifully.

Up early to drive back to London, we peer out of our French windows. The sky is red, the sun bright, the weir submerged, with the rushing river level on either side of it, and the lawns on the other side glassy with water.

As we leave the flat, I'm struck by this thought: the next time we walk in here, we'll be arriving to open the shows, and I'll have created Falstaff. My Falstaff. He doesn't exist yet, but he will then. It's the same feeling as when you start a book or a painting. The blank page, the empty canvas, the outline of a famous role. It's unimaginable that these vacant spaces can be filled in, and that a finished thing will appear...

Monday 6 January

London. Week two.

Filthy morning: windy, rainy, dark. The Victoria Line was closed, so we caught the Overground to Clapham. Erica Whyman (RSC Deputy Director) joined us so that she and Greg could have a catch-up on the way. *The top directors of one of the world's leading theatre companies are having a meeting strap-hanging on a train*, I thought, as I stared down the long, wet, swaying carriage, crowded with heavily wrapped people, many of them sniffing and coughing...

Trevor White (playing Hotspur) arrived in rehearsals. He's been on honeymoon in Burma. Face very tanned, with amazing green eyes shining out. For Trevor's benefit, Greg asked us to sum up some of the things we've learned about the material so far. I liked what Elliot Barnes-Worrell (playing Prince John and Francis) said: 'The plays are like all these windows... you see into all these lives... it's like Hitchcock's *Rear Window*.'

Then we worked on *Part I*, resuming the paraphrasing process. We're building up to a proper read-through of this part on Friday, when we'll finally read our own parts.

The thought of which sends a shiver through me.

Jim showed us a theatre programme today. From 1966. *Henry IV Part I*. A revival of the famous 1964 production, with Paul Rogers replacing Hugh Griffith, and Ian Holm still playing Hal. Jim told how he and Bobby (Hooper; twin brother; actor and writer) came to Stratford in a school party from Wolverhampton. It was the first piece of real theatre that they'd seen, and they marvelled at the ease with which the actors spoke Shakespeare, the authenticity of the costumes, even the stage smoke. 'It changed our lives,' Jim said; 'On the coach back, we said to one another, "That's what we're going to do!"' I was touched by the fact that Jim had a plastic folder round the programme, and he handled the pages very carefully, as if they were made of a precious substance. Which they were – memory.

Tuesday 7 January

Lunchtime. I had a meeting with a chap called Nick, a recovering alcoholic – he's a friend of one of the company – in an upstairs office at Clapham. A tall, strong man, aged fifty-six, he spoke very openly, the information tumbling out. Said it gave him goosebumps to remember what he'd been through. He's been sober now for eighteen years, but still gave me a very graphic demonstration of what it was like to start each day. (Which I'm thinking of using for a couple of scenes.) He explained that you'd have made preparations the night before: not only to have the first drink at hand, but also plastic bags, in case that first drink makes you throw up. 'You're putting poison into yourself – your body doesn't like it, but your nervous system needs it.' He showed me 'the shakes' – everything very tight and tense, the knees jumping, the hands flailing. How will you lift the drink? You mustn't spill any! Either bring your mouth to the bottle, while it stays on the surface, or one hand must help the other raise it. It could take him three hours to get ready for the day, and then people wouldn't notice a thing. 'The alcoholic is the consummate actor,' he said.

Other things that struck me:

'Alcohol is the father of all lies.'

'I'm not doing that again!' The cycle of resolving to clean up, but failing again and again. (Very Falstaff.)

'You're the host.' (Alcohol like a tapeworm.)

'Inner violence – an assault from within.'

At the end I thanked him earnestly. His honesty was moving, and he'd given me several things I could use.

Back in the rehearsal room, Greg said, 'I'm longing to hear what you found out.'

'I'll tell you later.'

'But it wasn't like the murderers?'

He was referring to my research for *Macbeth*, when I interviewed two real-life murderers, while he waited, nervously, to drive me home.

I smiled. 'No, it wasn't remotely like the murderers.'

Wednesday 8 January

First fat-suit fitting. With Bob Saunders, who is a speciality prop-maker, and this sometimes extends to costumes. He has made a rough version for me to try. Like a padded white diving suit, complete with arms and legs. I step into it, the rest is hauled up over me, and then zipped up the back. I look in the mirror. It works –

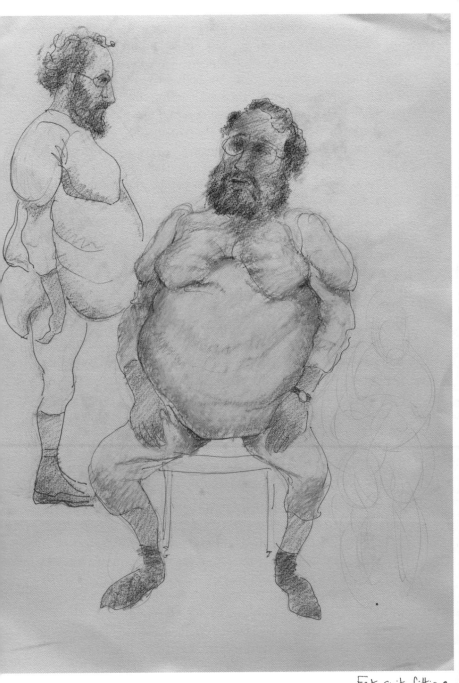

Fat suit fitting

immediately. With big sagging moobs, and an even bigger belly (both of these sections weighted), the overall impression is that it's *feasible* – I could, if I let myself go, end up looking like this. Stephen Brimson Lewis suggests some improvements, and I ask for a larger butt. Then I try sitting – good – the belly forces my legs wide apart. I try lying on the ground – good – I have to paddle my limbs like a beetle on its back in order to turn over and heave myself up. I try walking – good – a roll to my gait. We take photos – very, very good.

Just before I climb out of it, I remember to get my priorities right: 'How will I pee?' Bob says he'll have a think about it.

After he's gone, Stephen and I have a chat about the costume. I don't think there should be any vanity element. I've seen some photos of Robert Stephens in the part, and he had a bold, colourful, peacock look. That's definitely not for me. I want Falstaff to be much more dilapidated. Maybe he's homeless? Maybe Mistress Quickly lets him keep a trunk of belongings at The Boar's Head, but he mainly lives in the same clothes, and just sleeps in different taverns and bawdy houses. Stephen says he'll pick out a selection of old costumes from the RSC stores, and we'll try them on. We also have to think about his armour for the battle – very rusty, Stephen thinks – and then some change to his appearance in *Part II*, when he's playing out his fantasy of being the Hero of Shrewsbury, the Man Who Killed Hotspur.

In terms of make-up, Stephen reckons a wig might be best, to give my hair the bulk it needs to match the fat suit. And I want to try false eyebrows (like Ralph Richardson's, but more realistic), to help widen the face.

All in all, very exciting. I'm increasingly convinced that little Antony Sher can turn into big Jack Falstaff.

Afternoon. The historian Ian Mortimer came in to talk to us. He's the author of *The Time Traveller's Guide to Elizabethan England*, *The Time Traveller's Guide to Medieval England*, and *The Fears of Henry IV.* This latter book seeks to restore the reputation of Henry IV. Greg was quick to point out that it's not imbued with the same fervent zeal of the Richard III Society. Nevertheless, the book starts with this sentence: 'Shakespeare has a lot to answer for.'

Mortimer – a tall man with beaked nose and number-one crop on his dome – began by telling us that there is extensive information about Henry's life: 'His household accounts are so well preserved that we even know how he wiped his bum.' Then Mortimer delivered a fast, passionate account of his subject, meticulous about dates and details. In his youth, Henry was an exceptionally talented fighter (in jousts), 'the perfect knight'. As second in line to the throne, he decided to depose the tyrannical Richard II, and had him starved to death, which took two weeks. But once he was King, Henry had a run of bad luck: a series of harvest failures, which led to riots and rebellion. His worst problem was his own son – not the wastrel Hal of the plays, but more the character of Henry V, a born king, who couldn't wait for the crown.

I found all this interesting, but was more eager to plunder his knowledge of the times. And we're talking Elizabethan, not Medieval; Greg and Stephen want to set our production in the period when the plays were written.

Mortimer's description of drinking places was a surprise. At the top of the scale there were inns, which were like hotels, and relatively comfortable. Then taverns, which if they served wine, were still quite classy, then alehouses, then bawdy houses where you could still get a drink. He wasn't completely sure what sack was – my own research is proving difficult – but thought it was probably closer to wine than anything else. Which would make The Boar's Head posher than we've been imagining. Paola Dionisotti (playing Mistress Quickly) quite liked the idea, because her character has great pretensions, but I didn't. I said, 'I'd ask for my money back if I went to see the *Henries* and The Boar's Head was portrayed as a... a...'

Greg completed my sentence: '... A Premier Inn!'

'Exactly. I *want* it to be low life.'

Winding up the session, Greg said to Mortimer, 'You began by telling us that it's even known what Henry used to wipe his bum. What was it?'

Mortimer gave a little smile – *I got them with that one* – then answered, 'A kind of cotton wool.'

Thursday 9 January

The reviews for *Wolf Hall* and *Bring Up the Bodies* are ecstatic: they make front-page news on several of the broadsheets. 'I'm sure it's more Hilary Mantel than anything else,' Greg said; 'But it ain't half bad for the RSC!'

A bad attack of nerves tonight – about tomorrow's read-through. With two weeks' work already done, there's more need to deliver than normal. Yet why am I frightened – after forty fucking years in the job?! It pisses me off. Well, good, I'll get through it as I get through all pressurised situations – on *anger*.

Friday 10 January

…But no. I wake with an awful feeling of dread.

What's this about?

I suppose it's another aspect of being a character actor. A read-through presents us with a different challenge from most of the other actors. They can just read in their own voices. We have to suggest a completely different person – step into the spotlight with him, for all to judge.

And in this case I still feel a special focus on me – to prove I *can* play Falstaff.

Today is the moment that he makes his first appearance.

On the Tube journey, I find myself taking comfort from the thought of Meryl Streep filming *The Iron Lady*. There must have been days when, as an American, she had to stand up in front of a dozen distinguished British actors, and be Margaret Thatcher. That will have taken a lot of *chutzpah*, or balls, or call it what you will.

There's an emergency situation when we arrive (which helps distract me from my own anxiety): Jasper Britton can't make it. He's got gastro-enteritis. 'I wonder what he's wiping his bum with?' muses Sean Chapman (playing Northumberland and Douglas). Jasper's understudy, Simon Thorp, will read the part.

When it comes to Falstaff's first scene, I launch in with a voice that has gradually developed since that day when I pieced together his past: a bit posh, a bit fruity, a bit fatty.

People begin to respond well – with laughter – but what about Greg? This must be a big moment for him too. Whatever he might've said to the contrary, he went out on a limb when he cast me in this part. He's put his money down, as it were, and today he finally gets a glimpse of the goods. What if he doesn't like them?

At the end, he compliments us all on a splendid reading – which it was; people are doing exciting work – but I don't see him in private. He's swept away to lunchtime meetings, and then straight afterwards, we have the design showing: Stephen using a model box and screen images to reveal what the set will look like. It's a world of wattle-and-daub walls and rough timber floors, very simple and very flexible, effortlessly changing from Eastcheap tavern to Westminster court to Shrewsbury battlefield to Gloucestershire countryside. It's beautiful and striking. Stephen is very gifted.

Greg finishes today's work early, and it isn't till we're on the platform at Clapham North that he says to me, 'I thought your reading today was terrific.'

My heart lifts.

'And you've kept him completely hidden,' he adds. It's true. Throughout my line-learning I've made sure he never heard me doing any of the part. 'Where did that voice come from?' he asks.

I say I'm not sure – but later, thinking about it, realise it's an amalgam of the voices of two corpulent film actors from my youth: Robert Morley and James Robertson Justice. Both very self-assured, rather pompous, and with a sense of devilment. How the melting pot works...

There are moments in the creation of a role which are like growth surges: when you suddenly feel it developing, suddenly sense it could work. Today was one of those moments.

But it's still only the beginning.

Saturday 11 January

Over lunch at Frederick's, we were discussing the pleasure of working on Shakespeare's language, when Greg suddenly said, 'You know, I have the best job in the world!'

Monday 13 January

Week three.

In normal circumstances, we'd now start conventional, up-on-your-feet rehearsals; we've paraphrased the text and done the read-through. But these aren't normal circumstances. There's another whole play to go. So we were back round the table today, inching through *Part II*, doing what Greg calls these 'head-banging' sessions, and they were becoming quite, well, head-banging. But it's worth it. The clarity in last Friday's reading – you could *hear* it. And we'll break up this work with other activities during the week...

Tuesday 14 January

I asked my PA/researcher Sue Powell to help me find out about sack, and we're getting some conflicting information:

Onions's *A Shakespeare Glossary*: 'General name for a class of white wine formerly imported from Spain and the Canaries.'

Helen Hargest of the Shakespeare Birthplace Trust suggests it was a dry white wine mixed with sugar: 'Fynes Morrison in his account of his travels in England commented that he had never experienced seeing the practice of mixing wine with sugar in any other country, because "the taste of the English is thus delighted with sweetness".'

Cesar Saldana, Head of the Consejo Regulador (Regulatory Board) in Jerez, says: '"Sack" derives from the Spanish word "sacca" which refers to the quantity of wine drawn out from the "solera" (ageing stock) for shipment. The style of wine was probably a sweetened young oloroso. Somewhat similar to today's cream sherries.'

Nick King from the UK's Wine and Spirit Educational Trust says: 'Lustua (a current sherry producer) did until recently produce a wine called Dry Sack, which was a delightfully, slightly sweetened old oloroso.'

So – wine or sherry? I favour the theory that it's a dry white wine sweetened with sugar. (Falstaff refers to 'sack and sugar' in the tavern scene.) It's more feasible to drink that in great quantities than something like cream sherry.

Greg wants to show the company the battle scenes from Orson Welles's Falstaff film *Chimes at Midnight*: they're violent, messy, ugly. In searching for them tonight, we end up watching the whole film. I've seen it before, but it's different to what I remember. (Maybe because I know the material so much better now.) It's very handsome, in black and white, with rich use of chiaroscuro and those epic, low-angle shots which became Welles's signature style from *Citizen Kane* onwards. But despite its atmospheric darkness, it's surprisingly light in tone. Mainly due to Welles's own performance. It's as if he's so right for the role he forgets to play it. The result is, as *The New York Times* said in their review at the time, 'a street-corner Santa Claus'.

Orsen Welles as Falstaff

Wednesday 15 January

Our field-trip day: a company visit to the Museum of London and Westminster Abbey.

Can't say I was looking forward to it. I'm not a good tourist. When we go on holiday, there's a constant tug-of-war between Greg's desire to visit galleries, ruins and cathedrals, and mine to laze at the poolside with a good book and glass of chilled wine. There's something about hordes of bored people dutifully traipsing round a famous site that can kill it stone dead for me.

But today turned out to be different from that…

At the Museum of London, they'd prepared two private rooms for us, with artefacts and clothes from Elizabethan times. We were free to handle things, and there was an immediate thrill in being able to *touch* the past. Such surprising objects. From the large earthenware watering can to the tiny, delicately carved prod-and-spoon for removing ear wax. Many daggers; everybody carried one at the time. 'What would that do for your peace of mind?' mused Jim. One was called 'a bollock dagger', because of the shape of its handle. 'I've got to have that!' cried Tony Byrne, who's playing the violent, sexually crazed Pistol. Lots of drinking vessels – the kind that Falstaff would've used – made of pewter, clay and leather.

Most of the clothes had been recovered from being buried, so were a muddy brown. But the curators showed us a colour chart of the dyes available, and there was a rainbow of choices. A child's shoe was poignant, a codpiece drew giggles, and it was intriguing to see how things were repaired and adapted; your clothing was not as disposable as it is now.

They also had some theatrical items, which delighted us: the Hotspur costume worn by Charles Kean, and the bald wig, moustache and beard which George Robey used as Falstaff. They said they were puzzled by a pinkish, plastic-like film on the front of Robey's wig. 'It's his make-up,' exclaimed Stephen Brimson Lewis (who was soaking up all the details of the exhibits); 'It's still caked with his make-up!'

At Westminster Abbey we were surprised to be met by the Dean himself, the Very Reverend John Hall – bespectacled, straight-backed, with a cultured but twinkling manner. He led us to a place which features in *Part II*, Act Four, Scene Two, when the dying King asks:

KING HENRY IV: Doth any name particular belong
  Unto the lodging where I first did swoon?

WARWICK: 'Tis called Jerusalem, my noble lord.

KING HENRY IV: Laud be to heaven! Even there my life must
      end.
  It had been prophesied to me many years,
  I should not die but in Jerusalem,
  Which vainly I supposed the Holy Land.
  But bear me to that chamber. There I'll lie.
  In that Jerusalem shall Harry die.

The Jerusalem Chamber turned out to be a large, airy, panelled room hung with sixteenth-century tapestries. The Dean warned the squeamish among us not to look at the one behind me. I glanced round. It showed the circumcision of Isaac, and indeed I flinched. But most fascinating was the beamed ceiling: it bore Richard II's insignia. Which would have been the last thing seen by Henry IV (who, as Bolingbroke, deposed Richard), perhaps causing him to wonder if it had all been worth it.

I was expecting that to be the end of our visit, but now the Dean took us on a tour of the Abbey, with him as private guide. Although I'd been here several times before – and indeed had the honour to unveil the window to Marlowe in Poets' Corner a few years ago – this was special. The Dean led us up a little staircase behind the high altar, to the Edward the Confessor Chapel and Shrine, and then into a deeper space with Henry V's tomb. Alex Hassell bounded forward to touch it. The Dean told us that the carved figure originally had a silver head and hands, but these were stolen. The hands were only replaced in the last century, and modelled on Laurence Olivier's. Now the Dean fetched some keys on a wooden block, opened a door, and took us up another secret staircase – very narrow, with worn marble steps – into the Henry V Chantry Chapel where his wife Catherine was buried. This area had a marvellous, elevated view of the Abbey, and the whole building suddenly struck me in a new way. History was not dry, old and book-bound. History was alive, sensuous, heart-stirring. Seeing this colossal space, crowded with ghosts, seeing its long aisles and towering ceilings, half-dark in winter light, this was like seeing a natural wonder – the Victoria Falls or Grand Canyon – and it took my bloody breath away!

Thursday 16 January

When Greg went round the circle this morning, asking each person to comment on yesterday's field trips, the word most commonly used was 'moving'.

In the afternoon, a visit by James Shapiro, the Shakespeare scholar from New York (whom I last saw when we were there for the *Matilda/Caesar* openings). He has a very vivid way of talking about Shakespeare, or, as Greg put it, 'It's like they're episodes of *The Sopranos*.' Of Hotspur, James says, 'It gives me a rush watching him!' Of Falstaff: 'He frightens me, but I'm also envious of him. He symbolises an escape from the world of obligations. This man is Excess!'

He speaks about the *Henries* as the point in Shakespeare's writing career when he learns to meld History and Comedy. He describes Eastcheap as a green world – like the forests in *Midsummer Night's Dream* and *As You Like It* – a dreamworld, which doesn't quite exist. The first Falstaff/Hal scene begins with Falstaff asking what time it is, and Hal replying that it doesn't matter. And in their last scene – in *Part II* – when Hal rejects Falstaff, Hal says, 'I have long dreamed of such a man… but being awake, I do despise my dream.' But then again, James says, 'The whole of *Part II* mourns the loss of time, it is full of melancholy.'

Someone asks him about the Freudian aspect of Shakespeare. James suggests we might look at it the other way round. Did Shakespeare help to create Freud? The father of psychoanalysis read Shakespeare from an early age. Did he learn something about father/son relationships from Henry and Hal? Is there a better example of therapeutic role-playing than the 'play extempore' in the tavern scene? 'Cheaper than a session with your shrink,' says James.

Later, thinking about James describing Falstaff as 'Excess', I wonder if he'll be disappointed to see the character played as a real alcoholic, with drink making him suffer as well as rejoice? Some people want Falstaff to be just a pagan force, all-consuming and invincible. I'm saying no, let him have some very human fears about his health and his soul – Shakespeare has written these in, after all – and let him always disregard them.

But will that be acceptable to his fans?

Friday 17 January

Read-through of *Part II*. Like last week, I was full of nerves beforehand, and full of relief afterwards. Finally got to hear Jasper doing Henry, and he's going to be good (there you are, you see, I'm making judgements from a read-through): full of pain and fury. And Nia Gwynne (playing Doll Tearsheet) has a very heartfelt quality as an actress. This is valuable because Doll brings out a completely different side of Falstaff. Their relationship is strangely tender, and one of Shakespeare's masterstrokes in the writing: a fat old man with a pox-ridden whore. As for Oliver Ford Davies as Shallow – he stole the read-through just as he'll steal the show.

Saturday 18 January

Lunch with Ronnie Harwood. Good to see him looking pretty chipper. He's been through a lot. Two days after Natasha's funeral, he suffered a heart attack, and was operated on. Greg asked if he thought that the two things were connected. Ronnie replied, 'Of course. When they opened me up, they were looking for a broken heart.' He said he wasn't experiencing grief as he expected it to be, because he had a sense of Natasha being with him all the time. He regularly meets with Antonia Fraser and Victoria Rothschild (who was married to Simon Gray): 'We call ourselves the Three Merry Widows.'

Talked about Donald Wolfit playing Falstaff. It wasn't particularly successful, Ronnie said, and his padding was excessively big. As Wolfit's dresser, Ronnie had the grim task of trying to dry it out between performances.

'You'd better warn your wardrobe people,' said Ronnie.

'I will,' I replied: 'I'll tell them I've had a tip-off from Donald Wolfit's dresser.'

He said that when his hit play *The Dresser* was on, Ralph Richardson came to see it, and commented, 'Well, you've ensured that Wolfit will be remembered long after the rest of us aren't.'

Probably true. I was startled the other day when two of the younger members of the company asked me to identify the photos on the stairways of the Clapham rehearsal rooms. 'That's John Wood in *Sherlock Holmes*,' I explained; 'And that's Susan Fleetwood in *As You*.'

I felt like I was talking about actors from a different age.

Monday 20 January

Week four.

Worked on two of Falstaff's early scenes, the first one with Hal, and the robbery at Gad's Hill. I was expecting us to be on our feet, roughing them out, but we were still sitting in our chairs – playing our own parts, yes, talking about motivation, yes, but not staging anything. Normally I like hiding behind the table, and the script, for as long as possible, but not this time.

We need to be up.

We've only got seven weeks to go (I think).

For two plays.

I'm really quite worried.

Don't know whether to say anything to Greg.

Tuesday 21 January

Second fat-suit fitting.

Actually I'm getting to dislike the term – fat suit – it sounds like something you can buy off the rail at those plus-size shops. It's glib, it's cheapening, it's as unhelpful as that other term, Comic Role. I'm going to ban both of them. I'll say 'Falstaff's body suit' from now on.

Anyway, it was even better today, but quite a bit heavier. (What will this do to my back?) A useful discovery: it looked great on its own, but when we put clothes over it – just a shirt and trousers from stock – it lost all its detail, and was just like any old padding. The solution, we decided, was to make the clothes quite tight, so that the different shapes, like the moobs and belly, create their own clear folds, with distinct rises and falls.

In the afternoon, our fight director, Terry King, came into rehearsals, and we started to work out how to do the Battle of Shrewsbury. What weaponry, and so on. In fact, Shrewsbury was famous for the fact that it's the first time that English longbows were used on both sides. Otherwise, as Terry explained, the weapons varied from the broadswords and shields carried by the nobility to the pitchforks and staves with which Falstaff's 'scarecrow army' were armed. The most dangerous fighter is Douglas, and Sean Chapman wants to make him an SAS-type killer, working his way round the battlefield with lethal but unconventional weapons. Terry suggested a kind of club/hammer and slicing knives. Of course, Douglas has to kill Falstaff – apparently – and Greg wants to make this as convincing as possible. One of his favourite things as a Shakespeare director is what he calls Crossroads, injecting new tension into plot lines that are overfamiliar. What if you could convince an audience that things might go differently this time? Juliet might wake up in time, Macbeth might not do the murder, and indeed Falstaff might really have perished in the chaos of battle...

Wednesday 22 January

Good exploration of what we're calling 'the hangover scene' (*Part I*, Act Three, Scene Three): it could be early morning in the tavern – empty except for Falstaff and Bardolph still seated at their table; they haven't been to bed. I wonder if this is an opportunity to show Falstaff desperate for the first drink of the day? But, like on Monday, we could only *discuss* this – we couldn't try it out. And then that was me finished work for the day, and I went home. Of course, there are many scenes without Falstaff, and they need time too. But from a selfish point of view, I want to be rehearsing round the clock. I feel frustrated and a bit frightened. I must talk to Greg. But when? This week's schedule is already planned.

Thursday 23 January

The scarecrow-army scene (*Part I*, Act Four, Scene Two), when Falstaff describes how he exploits the press-ganging system, by accepting bribes from the best, most able recruits to be released from service, and substituting them with the dregs of humanity.

On my feet at last!

But my joy was short-lived. Greg was using the rehearsal to test out whether the limited number of actors available for my wretched army – most of them female – could create a constant stream of soldiers, by running round behind the set before plodding into view again, now as a different scarecrow person. It was a recipe for disaster. As I attempted to do the speech, everyone in the room began laughing at what was going on behind me: the Art of Coarse Acting run riot. This was upstaging on an industrial scale. I had to stop – I couldn't compete. Greg instructed the others to cut out all characterisation, and just be neutral figures. But the exercise was still hilarious. It'll be fine in performance – the army will be half-lit in the background, and you won't see them galloping round the back – but I don't know how we're ever going to rehearse it.

Friday 24 January

Morning. An archery teacher, Adrian Thomas, came in to talk to us about longbows, and to demonstrate – so that we can show them being used at Shrewsbury. He'd set up a target at the far end of the room, with padded protection around it. He asked for volunteers. Many of the guys, and gals, were up for it. Teaching them to aim, he made a fascinating observation. In everyday life, we aim all the time, effortlessly. 'Look at that exit sign,' he said: 'look at that tree out the window. You're doing it without thinking, spot on. But *try* and aim, and it goes wrong. Trust your subconscious, it's an expert – your conscious is an idiot. Get rid of the idiot, use the expert.' A good rule for creative work too, I think. Instinct is more reliable than intellect.

All week, the assistant director, Owen Horsley, has been rehearsing some the younger actors in a performance, which they showed the rest of us this afternoon. It was of *The Famous Victories of Henry V* by an unknown Elizabethan playwright: a popular feature in the repertoire of the Queen's Men company. We know they played in Stratford in 1587. Did the twenty-three-year-old Shakespeare see them do this piece? At any rate, he certainly knew it – the parallels can't be coincidental. The timescale of the action is from the Gad's Hill robbery through the death of the old King to the Battle of Agincourt and the wooing of Catherine. So basically both parts of *Henry IV* plus *Henry V* condensed into one play, and further condensed by Owen and his cast, who performed with great energy and humour. Some intriguing material. You see the 'box o' th' ear' which Hal gives the Lord Chief Justice – much referred to in *Part II* of Shakespeare's *Henries*, although (annoyingly) he omits to show it. And in the famous rejection scene, it's Poins who is spurned by the newly crowned Hal, not Sir John Oldcastle – the Falstaff figure here. I was astonished by the play. It was like seeing some sketches done by a minor artist, which inspired a genius to steal the ideas, improve and expand them, and produce three major works!

In terms of the box o' th' ear, Greg is thinking of 'doing a John Barton': lifting the sequence from *Famous Victories* and slipping it into the end of our tavern scene. He's also having to change the names of two characters, because they're confusing. The setter (a man who plans robberies) at Gad's Hill is called Gadshill – now he's Rakehell. And there's a Lord Bardolph in *Part II* – now he's Lord Randolph. When dealing with things like this – which seem like lazy writing – Greg will cry out, 'Oh, Shakespeare!', with the kind of exasperation you only feel for loved ones. (Meanwhile, Shakespeare himself had to change his original name for the Fat Knight, Oldcastle, to Falstaff, after complaints from the descendants of the real Sir John Oldcastle, a fifteenth-century proto-Protestant martyr.)

Saturday 25 January

If I wasn't in a relationship with my director, this is the moment I'd fire off a worried message to him or her. In the old days, it would've been by fax (I was quite notorious for my faxes), now it would be by email. Instead, after we'd breakfasted this morning, I said, 'Can I have five minutes? And can I break the house rules?' (We never discuss work at home.)

We went to his room, and I launched in. I said I felt we were already running out of time. And yet I hadn't properly started work on Falstaff. I could do an *impression* of him – his voice, his character – but it was like an outline, a cartoon. I have to find the real man. It's vital – otherwise the part can just consist of bluster.

Greg was thrown, even a bit shocked. He asked why I hadn't mentioned these anxieties before. I said they'd crept up on me during the week: times when I wanted to be playing scenes, not discussing them; times when I only rehearsed for a couple of hours in a whole day. 'And it's happening again on Monday,' I said, holding up the call sheet; 'We're doing my first scene for an hour and a half, and then that's it, I'm through.'

'There's a lot of other scenes to be...'

'I know, I know. I just wish we had more than three months to do this. I wish we had six months. They rehearse for six months on the Continent, why can't we here?'

'Because our budgets would never allow it.'

'Why not? You're running the company now – change the system. Why can they make it work in France, Germany, Russia, but we…'

'Because they get bigger state subsidies,' said Greg passionately; 'Because they value their theatre more! So don't talk to me about changing the system!'

'All right, all right, sorry,' I said, and we both caught our breath; 'Let's just carve out some more time… can we work evenings, can we work Saturdays?'

He said all that was possible, but wasn't necessary yet. He assured me that he had a big game plan mapped out, and that we *did* have enough time. 'And I promise you, when we get the scenes onto their feet now, you'll find the text *full*. The last four weeks haven't been wasted.'

'Of course they haven't. You know I don't think they have.'

We went quiet. He was looking lost. I didn't like seeing that. I regretted my little panic attack. The leading actor has to be as strong as the director, not just for the morale of the company, but for one another.

Later, he came down to my study/studio, where I was doing lines, and said, 'I feel I've let you down.'

'Not at all,' I said; 'I'm just ahead of myself. I've been working on the text for months – I need to *do* it now – but the others don't, they're not ready. Look, I shouldn't have mentioned it.'

'No, you *should*,' he said; 'You must always tell me how you're feeling.'

Monday 27 January

Week five. Which is now in Rehearsal Room Two.

Because the Roaring Girls season in the Swan needs more rehearsal space, we've had to move from Clapham. Greg was offered a variety of alternative places, and, not surprisingly, chose the Union Chapel in Islington, since it's just a few minutes' walk from our house. This will give him an extra hour and a half – our commuting time – each day, to do work on his other job, as Artistic Director.

The new room is much more characterful than the last one. It's huge and high, with an upper level, a three-sided balcony, and a beamed ceiling. Although it has tall windows, it's not a bright room,

Alex Hassell in rehearsals

so we have spotlights, and also the fierce yellow-red glow of several large heaters positioned around the acting area. These create a fireside atmosphere, but on a grand scale. There's something of The Boar's Head Tavern about our new home.

We start by staging – yes, on our feet, without scripts – the first Hal/Falstaff scene. Alex Hassell is happy with the idea of this being in a bawdy house, so that's how we're doing it. He's in bed with two prostitutes, they leave, and then I emerge from under some blankets on the floor. Alex is also happy to help me experiment with Falstaff's alcoholism:

He offers me a bottle of sack. My hands are shaking so badly, he has to take the cork out, and lift the vessel to my mouth. Later in the scene, when I become angry and resolve to 'give over this life', I pour away the contents. But then I cheer up, and when Poins enters with a new bottle, I greedily quaff away at it again.

I'm pleased to discover that all of this can work, without drawing too much attention to itself and taking over the scene. But I'm still just testing out the idea, just trying it step by step.

Alex never does the same thing twice as we rehearse the action again and again. This is an acting technique which I first encountered when I joined the Liverpool Everyman in 1972, and saw Jonathan Pryce in action. Although it wasn't natural to me, I liked it, and tried it, and indeed used it for many years. It's particularly useful if your character has to be dangerous and unpredictable – like, say, Leontes. But as I've got older, I've reverted back to the other way – where your moves are more planned and set – just as a safety mechanism. So Alex and I will have to find a way of negotiating our different methods, which is fine – actors do this all the time. I certainly don't want to restrict his instinct, because it gives Hal the energy of a big, irrepressible puppy, which is perfect for the beginning of the story.

Tuesday 28 January

The tavern scene (*Part I*, Act Two, Scene Four). Greg wants The Boar's Head to be as populated as possible, so the whole company are participating. Those who haven't got speaking parts and are extras (or 'warm props' as Jim says) must decide who and what they're going to be. Difficult for the women. A respectable lady wouldn't be here on her own, so are they servants or whores? It's been decided that Doll Tearsheet shouldn't be in this scene – we want to save her for *Part II*.

Greg: Now we don't want any 'wench acting'.

Nia Gwynne: We can't be Nancy in *Oliver!* then?

Greg: Definitely not.

Sean Chapman: Can I be the man peeing in the corner? In every print we've seen, there's a man peeing in the corner. Can I be him?

Greg: Definitely not!

Greg always says that directing is tyranny disguised as democracy. Today was a good example. He encouraged people to offer their ideas, and then started to rough out the action in a way that he'd probably already half-planned. It's a huge scene – lasting about thirty minutes – and a huge job to get it on its feet.

Sean Chapman in rehearsals (script page)

Wednesday 29 January

Each day begins with a group vocal warm-up, taken by Emma
Woodvine, who is a new RSC voice coach (recommended by Patsy
Rodenburg, one of the great voice gurus in the country, and now on
the RSC Board). Must say I'm very impressed. Emma has a relaxed,
and relaxing, manner, and radiates a sense of wisdom. This is essential for a voice coach in this company, because of course it's not just
about voice; it's about text, it's about Shakespeare. I love the sessions: half an hour of stretching, yawning (good for opening the
throat), humming, maa-may-moo-ing, percussive consonants, and
tongue-twisters. And then we finish with a favourite poem which
one of us has brought in. Today it was my choice. Philip Larkin's
'This Be The Verse'. There was something delightful about a
roomful of classical actors launching into the infamous opening line:
'They fuck you up, your mum and dad.' Emma pointed out that the
structure is like a nursery rhyme; it has a simplicity, an innocence,
that beguiles you into its subversiveness. Afterwards, she told me
that she'd been introduced to the poem by her *mother*.

I said, 'Clearly the message didn't work then.'

She laughed. 'No – she just said it could all be sorted out by good
parenting.'

Staged the hangover scene (*Part I*, Act Three, Scene Three), trying
the ideas we discussed last week. Early morning in the tavern; Falstaff in a foul mood and Bardolph patiently putting up with it. I felt
an immediate rapport with Josh Richards, and I think we're going
to be a good double act: Falstaff garrulous, restless, temperamental,
Bardolph deadpan, still, endlessly loyal.

Falstaff says, 'my skin hangs about me like an old lady's loose
gown.' Is this the shakes? Talks of how his life is 'out of all order'. I
think this is one of those moments of awareness, of horror, in an
addict's life. (I remember them from my cocaine days: the terrible
hangover I'd get after a session – I called it a coke-over.) In public,
and well-oiled, Falstaff can be the life and soul of the party. But in
private, at the end of a binge, and before starting another, he is
frightened, furious, blaming everyone else – in this case, Bardolph
– and determined to break the cycle. We've seen him like this before:
in the first scene, he says, 'I must give over this life', and blames Hal
for it.

Robert Stephens as Falstaff

Today we tried Falstaff roaming round the tavern, drinking the dregs from tankards left on the tables from last night. Then throwing it all away ('I'll repent, and that suddenly!'). Then accepting a fresh cup from Bardolph, and immediately feeling better: the shakes stop, his good humour returns.

So – again I find myself questioning whether it's okay to play a realistic portrait of an addict, including the struggle with himself.

I don't know if this has been done with Falstaff before; I've certainly never seen it. Robert Stephens could've brought that aspect to the role, but I don't remember any mention of it in the reviews. I never saw his performance. Which is just as well now, since it's regarded as the best of recent times.

Greg encourages me to keep exploring the idea, with one proviso – 'We can't fear for him, we can't sit there thinking, "If this man doesn't get to AA immediately, he's going to die!"'

Thursday 30 January

Stage management have brought piles of weaponry, jugs, caskets, bags, and all sorts from the RSC stores – to be used as rehearsal props until the real ones are selected. Today, Jonny Glynn (playing Warwick/Rakehell) dug out something from a heap in one corner, and said, 'Tony, isn't this yours?' I went over. It was one of the black crutches I'd used as Richard III. A bit dusty and scuffed, but unmistakably the thing itself. God. If I think of all the time and trouble that went into this object: the discussions about whether it was a very good idea or a very bad one – to play him on crutches – the tests to make them strong and safe enough. To say nothing of my investment in that role, my dreams and fears. (It's the story of my first book, *Year of the King*.) And here it is now, an old prop in a rehearsal room. A timely reminder as I attempt another of Shakespeare's great roles: it's not life or death; it's just theatre, which is ephemeral.

A little group of actors have gathered round the crutch.

Alex Hassell asks, 'What year was that?'

'1984,' I reply.

'Wow,' he says; 'I was only born in 1980.'

He gives a big, wonderstruck grin, while I think of one of Shallow's lines: 'Jesu, the days that we have seen!'

Friday 31 January

Coming from a dark, wet afternoon into our big, warm rehearsal room, with its firelit aura, and finding a fight call on the go – Hal and Hotspur bashing away at one another, the silhouette of Terry King circling and coaching – I felt I was walking into a jousting school from long ago.

For various reasons, like people's availability and costume fittings, we've moved on to *Part II*. Falstaff's first scene with the Lord Chief Justice. It's one of those scenes – and Falstaff has several – which can seem inconsequential on the page: just banter, not much story. But today we reminded ourselves that Falstaff is a criminal, a thief, and the Lord Chief Justice has the power not just to imprison him but hang him. As LCJ, Simon Thorp was icy and dangerous, and our exchange became full of tension, a dance on a tightrope. And probably funnier for it.

When rehearsals finished at six, Greg had no further appointments – which was unusual – so he was able to come home with me. We hurried through the rain and wind, having to wrap our umbrellas round our heads, and then, just a few minutes later, we were in our bright, heated house, and pouring glasses of our namesake drink.

Another week has ended, but now I have a much stronger sense of the plays working, and the performances working, my own included. The potential is really quite exciting…

Saturday 1 February

I've had lots of actors' nightmares during rehearsals – the usual thing, not knowing lines or being unprepared for a role – but last night I had a new one.

I walked into a theatre auditorium. A line of naked chorus boys were in front of me, horsing around roughly. I skirted past them. The director, a woman, hurried over to me. She said she was glad I was short and stocky: I'd invigorate the role, create it anew. 'Falstaff?' I said. She looked confused. 'No – Tarzan.'

Monday 3 February

Week six.

As I came into the bathroom this morning, the main section of the *Guardian* lay in front of the loo. Even from across the room, I could see the familiar layout they use when someone significant has died. Philip Seymour Hoffman. Born 1967, died yesterday of a drug overdose. God, he was only forty-seven. A seriously gifted man. His performance in *Capote* was as fine a piece of character acting as I've seen.

Each morning, after Emma's voice call, there's a singing call, for the company to learn the big Latin motet which begins *Part I*, 'Urbs beata Jerusalem', and the round in the tavern, 'Fill the Cup'. Everyone's joining in. Except me. I imagine Greg must have taken the Musical Director aside, and said, 'Tony has a little problem you should know about. In childhood he had the bar mitzvah teacher from hell, and it's left him with chronic tone-deafness.'

The scene we've called 'Fang and Snare' (*Part II*, Act Two, Scene One), where Mistress Quickly has hired two officers to arrest Falstaff for debt. Like in the scene with the Lord Chief Justice – who comes into this one too – we had to work hard to get some tension, some realism into it. I have a sense of Shakespeare dragging out comic situations and treading water in *Part II*, which is never the case in *Part I*.

Tuesday 4 February

…On the other hand, we did the Gloucestershire scene this afternoon (*Part II*, Act Three, Scene Two), where Falstaff visits Justices Shallow and Silence to recruit soldiers, and it's one of the most brilliant scenes in both plays, full of genuine comedy and strange melancholy ('We have heard the chimes at midnight'). It was good to have Oliver Ford Davies back in rehearsals – he's been absent for a week – and to watch him work. Such detail, precision, and invention. He has a gift for making Shakespeare sound spontaneous – searching for a word, a name, while keeping the rhythm of the text going. And of course a gift for comedy: he's developing a cackling laugh for Shallow – a sycophantic response to anything Falstaff says – and a shudder in one leg when he recalls the lust of his youth.

Singing call: Martin Bassindale, Rob Gilbert, Elliot Barnes-Worrell

Thursday 6 February

On the eve of the Sochi Winter Olympics, prominent authors from round the world have denounced Russia's anti-gay and other repressive laws. People like Günter Grass, Salman Rushdie, Margaret Atwood, Ian McEwan, Carol Ann Duffy, Wole Soyinka, Orhan Pamuk, Edward Albee, and many others. As appalled as I am by the homophobia in places like Russia and Uganda, I am equally heartened by the civilised world saying *no* to it.

Good work on Falstaff's hymn to alcohol, to sherry sack, in *Part II* (Act Four, Scene One). Took inspiration from Professor Robert Winston demonstrating the effects of alcohol in his 1998 TV series, *The Human Body*: using himself as the guinea pig, he drank through a bottle of red wine on camera, telling us what was happening inside. Falstaff does exactly the same. He gives us, the audience, a blow-by-blow account of how the sack is working on him; his brain, his voice, and – with the writing now becoming gloriously surreal – his bloodstream:

> …The sherry warms it and makes it course from the inwards to the parts extremes: it illuminateth the face, which as a beacon gives warning to all the rest of this little kingdom, man, to arm. And then the vital commoners and inland petty spirits muster me all to their captain, the heart, who, great and puffed up with his retinue, doth any deed of courage, and this valour comes of sherry!

The phrase, 'this little kingdom, man' is a perfect summation of Falstaff: he is a realm, a world unto himself.

And then the speech ends with Falstaff stating that if he had a thousand sons he'd get them all addicted to booze. My God, Shakespeare…! I can't wait to say that line in front of an audience.

Friday 7 February

With my lower back stiff and locked again, I visited Dr Rogers, the orthopaedic specialist whom I saw last year. He gave me biopuncture again – a series of injections in the affected area – which released the muscle spasm. I asked him about the Falstaff body suit. It weighs about six kilos. He thought it probably would affect my back.

I'm going to have to do something about it. Put health first, and sacrifice the fact that the suit gives me a feeling of Falstaff's weight without me having to act it.

Back at the rehearsal room, I reported to Greg and Suzi Blakey (our stage manager). We decided to try halving the weight of the suit. It was sent back to Bob Saunders for adjustment. And next week I'll try wearing it in rehearsals. Can't say I'm looking forward to it. The accoutrements of the part are starting to worry me:

I've been using a walking stick in the *Part II* scenes, after Falstaff complains of gout, and it's felt like an immediate cliché. Why? Don't know. In theatre, certain things just are. Not sure whether to persist with it.

And although the Falstaff voice sounded good at the read-throughs, now in the stop-start nature of rehearsals, it's starting to feel false.

I have to reassure myself that these things are in the nature of character acting.

This evening's TV news showed the opening ceremony of the Russian Winter Olympics. There were five giant snowflakes which unfolded into the five Olympic rings – except one malfunctioned and stayed closed. An American journalist said it was reluctant to come out.

Saturday 8 February

Greg has instituted Saturday rehearsals, mornings only. Mainly to give Mike Ashcroft (Movement Director) time to choreograph the action sequences: the Gad's Hill robbery, the attempted arrest of Falstaff by Fang and Snare, and, most challengingly, Pistol's arrival in the (*Part II*) tavern scene, when the character's manic energy unleashes chaos in the confined space of our one-room set. Snarling and slavering, producing dagger after dagger from his clothes, dropping his trousers, and swinging from a chandelier, Tony Byrne is creating a tour de force performance. Hair-raising stuff, which requires meticulous timing from us all. It's like learning a dance routine or a fight, you just have to do it again and again.

Tony Byrne rehearsing Pistol

Monday 10 February

Week seven.

Back in *Part I*. The tavern scene. We began to run it, and to my surprise Greg let it keep going – to get us past the hurdle, I suppose, of saying all the lines while doing all the action. But it was awful. I kept drying, could only half-remember the moves, and every detail vanished from what is a long, long scene. I was just adrift on a sea of Shakespeare with no land in sight. One of those times as an actor when you feel totally exposed and slowly crucified.

Anyway, we then worked through it, and some good things emerged.

Alex and I really began to click as actors. I went with his method – doing it differently every time – and it was absolutely right for the scene, which is like a prolonged improvisation. The best discovery was that Hal and Falstaff *enjoy* insulting one another:

> HAL: This sanguine coward, this bed-presser, this horseback-breaker, this huge hill of flesh –
>
> FALSTAFF: Away, you starveling, you elf-skin, you dried neat's tongue, bull's pizzle, you stock fish…

It's one of their games, and they relish the worst that the other has to offer.

(Note to myself: Falstaff needs to be thick-skinned. Stephen BL has observed that no other character in Shakespeare is described, physically, as much as Falstaff. But it's always abusive. At various times, he's called: 'fat guts', 'fat fool', 'fat-kidneyed rascal', 'swollen parcel of dropsies', 'stuffed cloak-bag of guts', 'whoreson candle-mine', 'whoreson, obscene, greasy tallow-catch', 'gross as a mountain', 'globe of sinful continents'. It's best for him to laugh along with these. Otherwise he could get seriously depressed.)

Afternoon. Wore the Falstaff body suit for the first time – a rehearsal version. They were supposed to have halved its weight, but it felt like there was none left at all. I put on an XXX-large T-shirt and sweat pants over it. There was a mirror on one wall, and the impression wasn't great. Without the big wig that'll I have, my head looked ridiculously small, and, as we'd already noted at the fitting, clothes make the shape seem generalised: any old padding. The other actors tried to make encouraging noises, but I wished they weren't seeing it like this. Normally in rehearsals, we all accept that any items of costume or props are only an approximation of the real thing. But it's somehow different with the body suit. I still feel the burden of *proving* I can play Falstaff. And that involves transforming myself physically. And the bloody body suit let me down today!

I must keep calm about it. The process is going to be like the Richard III crutches. We couldn't make them work at first – but we did in the end.

Thursday 13 February

Very enjoyable day. Greg had to assemble the Battle of Shrewsbury (the whole of Act Five), which became a technical exercise, with not much acting required. Which I like. Together with Terry King, Greg created a series of 'wipes', where a row of archers or a charge of scarecrow soldiers blur the action momentarily, allowing us to move to the next place of combat. Terry also fitted in the individual fights, which he's been rehearsing separately.

So the company got to see the Hal/Hotspur fight for the first time. Alex and Trevor have spent many hours practising, and it has paid off. They're both very fit and agile, the fight is long, fast and dangerous. What we saw today was halfway between dance and martial arts. Absolutely thrilling. I said to Terry King, 'You've created the best stage fight in the history of stage fights.' Which is what the story needs. When those two characters finally confront one another, you really want the sparks to fly.

As for Falstaff, I've completely abandoned the notion of him as a Vietnam vet, and rejected Harold Bloom's emphasis on him being a soldier. There's far more mileage in playing a fat old man who shouldn't be anywhere near a battlefield. While people are fighting and dying all around him, he complains of the discomfort ('I am as hot as molten lead'), disparages the value of honour ('I'll none of it'), and saves his skin by playing dead ('Time to counterfeit').

Have to confess that our image of him at Shrewsbury is half borrowed from Welles's *Chimes at Midnight* film, where the Fat Knight is seen puffing round the edges of the battle, like Pooh Bear in armour, looking for somewhere to hide.

Hal/Hotspur fight

Friday 14 February

Less enjoyable day. Much more nerve-wracking. We worked through the whole of *Part I*, not running it continuously, but scene by scene. Greg asked us to wait in another room when we weren't in the scenes, to take away the pressure of performing in front of one another. This helped a little, but on the other hand some of the creative team were present – Stephen Brimson Lewis, Tim Mitchell, Paul Englishby – so there was an audience of sorts. There was also the production photographer taking rehearsal shots. I didn't put on the body suit – it would *not* photograph well – and just wore my big winter coat to give myself some bulk.

Anyway... some of the work was generalised, but a lot of it felt good. I was okay: drying more than I would've liked, but Falstaff himself became clearer. Despite everything I've said about it not being a Comic Role, the character I'm creating – posh and pompous, yet vulnerable – *is* making people laugh, and the situations themselves are undeniably funny. As is Falstaff's outrageousness: his version of what happened at Gad's Hill, his claim to having killed Hotspur. So if he's to be a real, three-dimensional man, I'm going to have to focus more on his darker, more melancholy side. His fear of damnation is surprising – for such a pagan creature – but it's certainly there, a deep-seated thing, probably rooted in childhood. And his fear of ageing and mortality – that surfaces more in *Part II*, but I must thread some of it through *Part I* as well.

But all in all, it was another of those growth-surge moments, when you feel a performance taking shape, feel it starting to work.

At the end, we all sat in a circle, in the fireside glow of that room, with blue evening light in the windows, and discussed the day. Greg said, 'It's an extraordinary play. It's like a classy variety show, with all these different acts, *so* different – Falstaff's world, Hotspur's world, the King's world – and we relish them all, and they keep coming back. Extraordinary!'

As we broke for the weekend, I noticed that several members of the cast had popped out to buy flowers and were taking them home. It's Valentine's Day. Greg and I had left cards on one another's desks this morning, both signed 'Anonymous'.

Monday 17 February

Week eight.

Worked on *Part II* (aiming for a stagger-through next week). It was strangely unfamiliar. That keeps happening, with both plays. You go back to one or the other, and it's like you're just starting again. Which is unnerving at this stage of rehearsals, when, in normal circumstances, everything would be feeling more and more secure, comfortable, second nature. Oh, I wish we had more time…!

Evening. To Buckingham Palace. For a celebration of RADA. Founded by Sir Herbert Beerbom Tree in 1904. With the Queen as Patron since 1952.

We went by taxi, with an official sticker in the window, which allowed us to join the queue of cars outside the gates. The security checks took for ever, and then we were finally driven into the courtyard and the front entrance.

This was a peculiar occasion for me. When I arrived in London in 1968, I auditioned for the top drama schools, and was turned down, first by Central – with that little run up their steps, and the run back down, empty-handed – and then, more harshly, by RADA. Their letter said: Not only have you failed this audition, and not only are we unable to contemplate auditioning you again, but we strongly urge you to seek a different career.

I told this to everybody I met this evening – 'I was a RADA reject' – until one of them, Mike Leigh, said to me cheerfully, 'Tony, will you shut up about that. Nobody gives a shit.'

(He was quite right. The only person who did give a shit – the shocked nineteen-year-old from South Africa – no longer existed, and nor did his saviour, his mother, who said they were wrong.)

So then I gave myself over to the evening, which boasted an impressive array of British theatre talent: playwrights like Stoppard, Hare, Hampton, and my cousin Ronnie H, directors like Trevor Nunn and Terry Hands, actors like Alan Rickman, Richard Wilson, Peter Bowles, Tom Courtenay, and some that were surprising RADA graduates – Roger Moore, Joan Collins, and Angela Lansbury.

Before the event itself, we were invited to greet the Queen. I was pleased to discover that her special handshake was undiminished since the time of my knighthood in 2000. On that occasion, when we were being briefed beforehand by the Master of the Household, one of us asked how we'd know when our time with Her Majesty was over, and he answered enigmatically, 'Oh, you'll know.' It turned out that after the sword-dubbing and a little chat, she extended her hand, you took it, and she gave you a polite but firm shove to the side. As tonight.

We gathered in the Throne Room, on the rows of seats set out there. Then she entered. It was extraordinary how one little old lady could silence several hundred noisy theatricals.

The show was short: a couple of scenes from plays, a couple of musical numbers. It then needed a great tribute to RADA, but the man best suited to deliver it, the school's President, Richard Attenborough, was too ill to attend, so instead his brother David just said a quick thanks on his behalf.

Helen Mirren finished proceedings by doing 'Our revels now are ended' from *The Tempest*, while the rest of us sat wondering whether the Queen had ever seen *The Queen?*

As we were leaving, we bumped into Terry Hands. He told us that when he directed the *Henries* in 1975, he offered Falstaff to Olivier, who declined, saying, 'Oh no, it's Rafie's role.' (Meaning R. Richardson.) Then, giving that slightly wicked smile of his, Terry assured Greg that I was up to the part: 'After all, he's one of the most inventive actors in the country.' Which you could read in different ways...

Tuesday 18 February

The two boys who are to play the Page arrived: Luca Saraceni-Gunner and Jonathan Williams, both aged ten, both from Stratford. The law states that any child's part has to be alternated, and they have to be accompanied by a chaperone at all times.

We put them into their scenes, which meant running each of these twice. With everything a bit mechanical, I felt exposed again: the Falstaff voice, and, worse, the Falstaff suit. I don't know what to do about this. Wearing it, or rather seeing myself in the mirror, makes me dispirited – it looks bad – yet I have to keep rehearsing with it.

Working with kids is not my favourite thing – they can be distracting to an audience, and difficult to hear – but these two were good today. So at least that was heartening.

As was a letter that I received this morning – by complete chance, it was from someone who'd been one of the boys in *Cyrano* back in

1997. Now an adult, and a musician, he'd just finished reading my autobiography, *Beside Myself*, and was writing to say that he'd enjoyed it, and that *Cyrano* had been 'a thrilling formative experience'.

I was touched by his letter. But it also brought to mind a terribly embarrassing incident during the tour of *Cyrano*. In Blackpool. I'd come into the wings, preparing to enter. Cyrano's first scene is long. My tummy felt rather bubbly, so I went to the deepest, darkest corner of the backstage area, and adopting the classic stance – half-bending, making fists – let rip with a big one. Moving away, I glanced back, and, with my eyes now adjusted to the dark, saw the children's chaperone seated there, her face exactly level with where I'd aimed my fire. Her expression was of shock. I realised that from her POV, my action might have seemed deliberate – seeking out that particular spot. There was no way of apologising or explaining. I imagined people asking her what I was like, and her answering, 'Well, he seemed a decent enough chap, but then one evening…!'

Thursday 20 February

Costume fitting. I put on the rehearsal body suit for Stephen BL to see. He immediately detected the problem. They had accidentally removed all the weight, leaving it with the substance of a big feather pillow. Even tying the cord on the sweatpants caused the belly to bulge up, and now Falstaff's chief feature was a barrel chest. Stephen promised to solve the problem with Bob Saunders. I changed into the actual body suit, and, despite the weight, it was a relief to see it looking convincing again. There weren't many real items of my costume – they were trying out different cuts, shapes and materials – except for a great, dun-coloured leather coat. Broad, long, battered with age, it had something of the Wild West to it (the real one, not Hollywood's version), and for me it was love at first sight. This will be Falstaff's main silhouette.

In rehearsals, we did the final scene, when Falstaff approaches Hal after his coronation, and Hal rejects him: 'I know thee not, old man.' Greg staged a grand formal procession, with Hal being the last on. Alex tried a version where he broke out of the line, to shake the hands of onlookers. Afterwards, Greg used our visit to Buckingham

Palace to talk about the power of majesty: how the Queen had
silenced the Throne Room just by entering it, how there was an aura
around her that was almost palpable – an unbreakable glass bubble –
and although we had shaken her hand, the impression was of her
being untouchable. We did the scene again, and now Alex was mag-
netically fixed into the ceremonial parade. It was infinitely better.
Falstaff's intrusion was seriously out of order.

Tuesday 25 February

Week nine.

I had most of today off. Used it to go through all the lines – both
parts. I can rattle through them faultlessly, alone in my studio/study,
but in rehearsals they still keep slip-sliding away. Not badly, just the
odd word or two, but it bugs me. It's like I said before: it's not
enough to know lines, you have to know them under pressure. And
although rehearsals themselves aren't real pressure, constantly alternating the two plays is.

Wednesday 26 February

Greg had to go in early for a meeting. I found this note on the
kitchen table:

'We are on! Rebecca very pleased.'

Translated, that means the Arthur Miller Estate have approved
Greg as director of *Salesman*, and Miller's daughter has personally
endorsed it.

The irony is that Greg wasn't supposed to do this one. Our
favoured choice, a very prominent director, was rejected by the
Estate. No reason given. They can be quite sinister, these Estates.

Anyway, so Greg has stepped into the breach, rather like I did with
Falstaff.

When I got to rehearsals, preparations were under way for our first
run – no, stagger-through – of *Part II*. I said to Greg that the *Salesman* news had given me a boost of confidence: 'If we fuck up these
shows, at least we know we've got another.'

The stagger-through differed from the previous one, in that,
although we stopped briefly between scenes, we basically kept it
going, and we were allowed to watch the sections that we weren't in.

Greg directing

Always a big moment. It can feel like your colleagues sitting in judgement on you. But ours is a warm and supportive company, and there was much laughter. Of course, rehearsal laughs are notoriously unreliable and misleading – a real audience might not find the same things funny at all – and some directors discourage them. (Nick Hytner came close to banning them during *Travelling Light* rehearsals.) Anyway, they were pretty encouraging today.

The play itself is a strange beast, very different from *Part I*, which has a much tighter, more exciting structure. In our discussion afterwards – our tribal conference by firelight – Jasper said that he found the piece Chekhovian: the drama being in the detail and the humanity, rather than the storyline. Others commented on how the lack of narrative drive reflects an England ruled by a sick, faltering king. Paola said it was 'a hymn to individuality'.

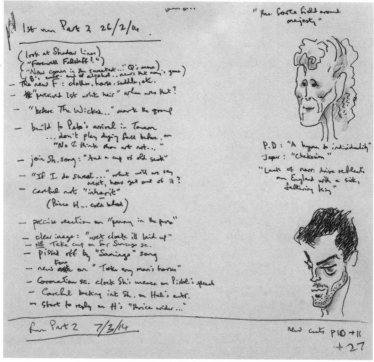

Paola D. x Alex H. (script page)

Friday 28 February

Back in *Part I*, good progress on the big tavern scene, particularly the 'play within the play'. We plotted in responses for the onstage audience: the named characters like Bardolph, Quickly, Poins, etc., and all the unnamed ones who are Boar's Head guests or staff. They have to laugh, cheer, groan, echo some lines, ad-lib others, and all these have to be as fixed and reliable as any other cues in the show. This takes a lot of practice, but it's worth it. Otherwise, they may be fine today, but when we come back to the scene in a week's time, everyone will be a little hesitant, and leave it to everyone else to make some noise. Which can result in total silence.

I noticed a line at the end of this section, which relates back to Falstaff's history (the story of his grandfather's ring). The Sheriff is knocking at the door, breaking up the party – he's accompanied by guards, and intends to search the premises. Do they let him in? The loot from the Gad's Hill robbery is inside, as are the perpetrators. The danger of capture and punishment is real. Falstaff dares Hal to allow the Sheriff to enter, saying, 'If I become not the hangman's cart as well as another man, a plague on my bringing up!' There's an acting choice here. You could send up the line, with Falstaff playing at mock-heroics (in the manner of, 'It is a far, far better thing that I do'), or you could play it for real, with Falstaff reminding everyone that he has been raised as a gentleman, and if his time is up, he'll go to the gallows with dignity.

I'm choosing this second way.

A good find.

Sunday 2 March

It's here. An unmistakable new feeling in my body – in my belly mostly – connected to the new month, and the fact that over the next four weeks we'll be doing run-throughs, dress rehearsals, and previews of the plays. The feeling is a curious mixture of excitement and dread. I think sportsmen and athletes must know it. Certainly any actor who's played any of Shakespeare's great roles will be familiar with it, while people who call us *luvvies* won't have a clue what I'm talking about. I would *luv* to make one of those people learn a part like Falstaff, and I would *luv* to stand next to them in the wings before their first entrance – and I would *luv* to clear up whatever mess they leave on the floor behind them.

Monday 3 March

Week ten. (Our last in London.)

I'm let off rehearsals this morning for a special event at Westminster Abbey: the Memorial Service for Nelson Mandela.

The great and the good are here, including Prince Harry (the real one), the leaders of the Government and Opposition – Cameron, Clegg, Miliband – and the Archbishops of Canterbury and York. Proceedings are led by the man who gave us a private tour of the Abbey a few weeks ago – the Dean, John Hall. But the show itself is stolen by two South African visitors. First, the Soweto Gospel Choir, who, dressed in T-shirts and jeans, sing traditional numbers – hearing them in this majestic British cathedral touches my heart. Second, Desmond Tutu, who gives the main address. A bit frail now and quite bald, he is still the most skilful of orators. He knows it's good to begin with a laugh, so he tells us that in the bad old days of Apartheid, there were road signs saying, 'Drive Carefully – Natives Cross Here', and that, during the period of unrest which led to the new democracy, someone changed it to: 'Drive Carefully – Natives Very Cross Here'. And he knows the power of repeating a key phrase – in this case, 'Thank you.' He whispers it, warbles it, praising various British figures who fought Apartheid, then says it louder, more passionately: 'Thank you, God, for Madiba!'

The morning's proceedings end with the South African anthem. I, who've stood silent during the singing of hymns – my excuse being that I'm tone deaf *and* Jewish– now join in gamely, being one of the few in this congregation who can pronounce both the Xhosa part – '*nkosi sikelel'*' – and the Afrikaans – '*uit die blou van onse hemel*'. The latter rang like a Nazi marching song through my childhood. Today it brings tears to my eyes. Its inclusion in the anthem of the New South Africa typified Mandela's spirit of reconciliation. The man himself would have been amazed and humbled, I think, by this service in this place – the first ever for an African leader.

Tuesday 4 March

Morning. Wig fitting. Sandra Smith in charge, down from Stratford. My longest friendship at the RSC is with her. Welsh, warm, funny, she joined the company just after me – as a junior wiggy (wig and make-up assistant). Today she runs the department. The Falstaff wig is a wild mass of grey curls, with a yellowish tinge (tobacco smoke or dirt?), and it's very promising. It broadens my whole head. Stephen BL also produced a big-brimmed leather hat which was full of character: beautifully aged and bashed, curling at the edges, with a chunk missing, and greenish stains here and there. It's a bit cowboy – so it'll go perfectly with the coat – and also a bit Don Quixote. Which is apt. Falstaff – the old knight, the old fantasist.

Sandra Smith knotting a moustache

Afternoon. Wore the body suit in rehearsals, the real one. It's now about three kilos. There's a definite discomfort factor – the heaviness and the heat – but the advantages outweigh it (no pun intended), and I could finally look in the mirror without cringing.

The wits were out. As I waddled past Simon Thorp, he said, 'Tony, when *are* you getting your fat suit?' And Keith Osborn (playing the Archbishop), to whom I'd just confessed that I'd had a McDonald's lunch, said, 'Tony, is that really just one Big Mac?'

Wednesday 5 March

Run of *Part I*. Did it in the body suit and it felt okay (you get used to the weight and forget about it), as did my performance. And the lines too – they were mostly there. I think I fret about them too much. Jasper's attitude to line-learning is diametrically opposite to mine – he says he can't learn them before rehearsals, or indeed before he's fully understood the character. So a run-through situation like today was very difficult for him. But neither he nor Greg seemed remotely worried. It's just a different work method.

Thursday 6 March

Run of *Part II*. Jasper knew his lines perfectly, and the Jerusalem scene was tremendous. The King is described as 'the lion', and that's how Jasper is playing him, but an old, wounded lion, roaring against the dying of the light. And Alex has grown into the best Hal imaginable, effortlessly able to play the two conflicting sides of the character: the wild boy with his surrogate father, and the strong, heroic future king with his real one.

Meanwhile, for me, the unfamiliarity of the play – we haven't done it for a while – suddenly made me feel uncomfortable in the role. It's those early scenes, first with the Lord Chief Justice, then Mistress Quickly. We thought we'd solved them – put more tension into the confrontations – but the writing keeps pulling us back. Falstaff is simply not the complex character of *Part I*: he's come back in the sequel to please audiences, and he's doing a series of turns, holding forth about this or that, wriggling out of tricky situations, but he's like a lightweight version (no pun again) of himself – more like the Falstaff of *Merry Wives*. Later in *Part II*, the real man emerges – as in the

Jasper Britton in rehearsals

scene with Doll Tearsheet – a man frightened of ageing and death, but this came as a jolt to me today, my performance wasn't ready for it; one minute I was in *Merry Wives*, the next *King Lear*. Those early scenes threw me. I was *trying* to be funny. Fatal. By nature I'm not a comic actor, so I just felt false. This is the worst thing – feeling false.

It's the *real* challenge of character acting. You're performing a magic trick: here before your very eyes, Antony Sher will vanish and John Falstaff will appear! This illusion will be achieved not by the voice I assume or the padding I wear, but by the strength of my own conviction. It's a very powerful thing. I can make you believe that I am Falstaff – as long as I believe it myself. And today I didn't...

This was the wrong time to have a crisis. Tomorrow is our last day in London, and we're running both plays – running the marathon.

At the end of rehearsals, I asked Greg if we could stay behind for a talk. I outlined the problem. He responded in a way that he could only do with *me* – a frankness that he wouldn't use with other actors:

'You're exaggerating.'

I bristled. 'Oh, am I?'

'Yes, you're overreacting.'

'Well, that's in my job description.'

He gave a brief smile – it's one of our old jokes – then went on: 'It didn't *show*, what you're saying. You were good in those early scenes – though God knows they're not Shakespeare's best writing – and from then on you were more than good.'

'So why did it feel like the opposite?'

'Because you got off to a bad start, or you felt you had.'

'So what do we do about me *feeling* I'm getting off to a bad start?'

'We make you more comfortable in those scenes...'

We then had a discussion about finding more meat in them, more for me to get my teeth into, more than just the hot air of bluster. Greg pointed out that there were two aspects of Falstaff which I could explore further in the opening sections. One, his *health* – he's worried about it, he's had the doctor examine his urine, he complains of gout, he fears he has the pox. Two, his *fantasy* – he's trying to play a new role, the Hero of Shrewsbury, he's buying new clothes, a new horse, he claims to have some official post in 'this land service', and to be 'upon hasty employment in the king's affairs'. In his exchanges with the Lord Chief Justice, Falstaff is seeking to put himself on the same level as someone of real importance.

Greg did an effective job. By the end of our discussion, I was excited to try out these new things, eager to do the scenes again.

Friday 7 March

A big day. Running both plays. The summation of our work so far.

As we left the house, Greg quoted Falstaff before the Battle of Shrewsbury: 'I would it were bedtime, Hal, and all well.' But I sensed he was secretly excited.

In the morning, the run of *Part I* was terrific. One of those times when a company of actors is like a sports team, which has been in training, has grown totally fit, has finally to play the big match, and does so at the top of their form. From a personal POV, I was flying…

In the afternoon, *Part II* was not as terrific. Although I felt much better in the early scenes, nothing seemed to really ignite till the tavern scene, with Pistol and Tearsheet, and from then on it was a peculiar mixture of brilliant scenes (Shallow/Silence, the Jerusalem Chamber, Hal's rejection of Falstaff) and some that were rather flat. It's the play itself, I fear, and there's not much we can do about that.

Anyway, generally speaking, we're in extremely good shape, and the company's work is first rate. Quite apart from what the principals are doing, there's also some fine character acting going on: Josh's double as Bardolph and Glendower, Sean's deadly Douglas, Jonny's seedy Rakehell, Martin Bassindale's pipsqueak Peto, the wretched recruits in the Gloucestershire scene: Jonny again, Simon Yadoo, Leigh Quinn, Nick Gerard-Martin, Youssef Kerkour… I could go on and on…

As for myself, I got some nice compliments from the VIPs who were watching – Jeremy Adams, John Wyver, and Robin Lough (director of the Live broadcasts) – and allowed myself to briefly fantasise about this part turning out well for me. A success in a great Shakespeare part – there's nothing like it.

On a more mundane level, I wore the body suit throughout, and it was bearable – as long as I sat down in-between scenes, and drank lots of water. As for the lines, I never had to ask for a prompt, and, even if I spoke garbage at times, I *kept going*.

John Gielgud once said, in typically indiscreet fashion, that the good thing about playing Shakespeare is that if you forget your lines you can just make them up, since no one understands what you're saying anyway.

(I don't think Greg would approve…!)

Today was the last day in the Union Chapel rehearsal room. At the end, we all gathered on the upper level, poured some Prosecco into plastic cups and Greg proposed a toast to our stage managers. Suzi Blakey leads a crack team: Klare Roger, Daisy Gladstone and Charley Sargant. They now began a Herculean task, packing all the furniture, props and costumes into huge boxes. I thought of the hours they've spent in this room, arriving long before us each day and leaving long after we've gone. And the hours we've all spent together on the work, sometimes exciting and joyful, sometimes tense and frustrating. Because you put everything you've got into a show, at this stage you will always feel it's going to be a hit. You will feel this even with shows that turn out to be flops. For now you are blind with good intentions, positive thinking, and hope. So it's impossible to predict the outcome reliably. And so creativity remains a game of chance.

Saturday 8 March

Packing for Stratford was difficult. I'm going to be away for a long time, about seven months. Along with the task of remembering everything that I might need, there was that sadness which afflicts me whenever I make a big move, and which I try to joke about: 'He's here,' I said to Greg; 'The Wandering Jew is here again.'

It was a beautiful day to make an important journey: soft sunshine and spring blossom coming out.

When we reached Avonside and climbed out of the car, we both took a deep breath. The smell of woodsmoke, the river, and countryside. Greg remarked that one of his favourite lines in the plays is when Justice Shallow says of his Gloucestershire home, 'Good air!'

Sunday 9 March

How splendid to be able to begin the day with a river walk again. The weather was spring-like, the Avon sparkling under a perfectly blue sky. Near the weir at Lucy's Mill, we saw the big male swan which we call 'the mad one'. He has a strange attraction to kayaks, mimicking their motions, turning when they do, and sometimes getting randy with them, which must be quite alarming for their occupants.

Down the other end, we crossed at Clopton Bridge, then, instead of looping back towards home, we detoured to the famous Gower Memorial: the statues of Shakespeare and four of his characters. Greg pointed out that two of these were from the *Henries*: Falstaff and the one which everyone thinks is Henry V, but is in fact Hal trying on the crown. The sculptor, Lord Ronald Gower, was a friend of Oscar Wilde's (who attended the unveiling in 1888), and also gay –

he got into trouble for trying to pick up a guardsman at Buckingham Palace. Though I don't think you'll find that in the guidebooks to Stratford-upon-Avon.

Monday 10 March

Week eleven. And Rehearsal Room Three.

The Michel Saint-Denis Studio at the Courtyard Theatre. (Named after one of the most innovative directors of the last century, whom Peter Hall recruited as an artistic adviser in the early years of the RSC.) A big, square, airy space, it holds a lot of good memories for me; I rehearsed *Tamburlaine*, *Roman Actor* and *Malcontent* in here.

Quite a light day. A long note session on *Part II*, and rehearsals of a few scenes. We'll carry on working *Part II* tomorrow, and then our focus switches onto *Part I* full time, because we actually start teching it on Friday.

Greg and I popped into the theatre at lunchtime, and saw the set going up. We were in the Upper Circle, and down below was an army of stage crew with hard hats and radio controls. It looked very serious. A far cry somehow from learning lines in my little rooms, or even what's been going on in rehearsals. This was an epic image of people preparing for a world-class theatre event. It's easy to forget the scale of it. And you have to forget it, in a way.

Tuesday 11 March

Rehearsal of the second tavern scene, during which the drunkenly crazed Pistol stands on the table, holding the ends of the long tablecloth, which is wrapped round Falstaff, Doll, Bardolph and the Page. Their lunging movements suggest galloping horses. Pistol misquotes a line from *Tamburlaine*: 'And hollow pampered jades of Asia.' In Marlowe's actual play, Tamburlaine is in a chariot drawn by the kings he's conquered, and cries, 'Holla, ye pampered jades of Asia!' This morning I realised that by pure chance I was in exactly the same spot in the same rehearsal room as when I did the chariot scene as Tamburlaine in 1992. Who would've ever thought that I would be back here twenty-two years later, now in a Shakespeare play, with one of the other characters satirising Marlowe?

Ah, the whirligig of theatre…

I must say that the piece of action we've created to end the scene feels absolutely right. Falstaff and Doll can't bear to part, yet their words of farewell are clumsy and inadequate. As written, Falstaff and Bardolph then exit, and a moment later Bardolph calls Doll from offstage: 'Come to my master.' Mistress Quickly urges her, 'O, run, Doll, run,' and Doll exits. What's happened? It can't be that Falstaff has just slipped and fallen over. It has to be more significant. So we're showing Falstaff and Bardolph outside the tavern. Suddenly Falstaff breaks down. Bardolph hurries back in to summon Doll. She runs into Falstaff's arms and they embrace deeply. Theirs has been a love scene (albeit one of the most curious love scenes ever written), and this is a fitting end to it.

We ran *Part II*. It was seven minutes shorter than last Friday's run, and generally much better.

I must just report – for the record – that when we got to the Shallow/Silence scene in today's run, everyone in the room stopped whatever they were doing to watch Oliver Ford Davies give a Masterclass in Comedy Acting. I don't know which was more joyful – Oliver's performance or the company's delight in it. And Jim is proving the perfect foil as Silence: a character lost in some deep, inner place. Imbued with this spirit, he joins Shallow in a section which makes you question whether the author is William Shakespeare or Samuel Beckett:

> SHALLOW: …O the mad days that I have spent. And to see how many of mine old acquaintances are dead.
>
> SILENCE: We shall all follow, cousin.
>
> SHALLOW: Certain, 'tis certain, very sure, very sure: death is certain to us all, all shall die. How much a good yoke of bullocks at Stamford Fair?
>
> SILENCE: Truly cousin, I was not there.
>
> SHALLOW: Death is certain. Is old Double of your town living yet?
>
> SILENCE: Dead, sir.
>
> SHALLOW: Dead? See, see, he drew a good bow, and dead?

And then Silence blossoms bizarrely in Act Five, Scene Three when he's drunk and can't stop singing. Shakespeare is renowned for his

Jim Hooper and Oliver Ford Davies rehearsing Silence and Shallow

colossal portraits of mankind, like Lear, Hamlet, Falstaff, and so on
– drama's equivalent of Michelangelo's marble giants – but with
someone like Silence you also see what a superb miniaturist he is.

Today was the last we'll see of *Part II* for a fortnight (while we open
Part I). It's a mind-boggling thought.

Thursday 12 March

There's fog on the river, which is beautiful, and tension in my belly,
which is not. It's the final day of rehearsals. A run of *Part I* this afternoon...

The morning was taken up by technical work – not much acting
required. Paul Englishby had brought the band in, and we tried
some of his music cues. Including the tune which the tavern musicians, Sneak's Noise, play during Falstaff and Doll's scene. It had
just the right bittersweet air to it. Then Paul tried a slow, strange,
drumming accompaniment to the march of Falstaff's ragged soldiers
in the scarecrow-army scene, and now Nia had to stop playing Doll
and become one of them. This procession has never ceased to
upstage me, and this morning was no exception. Greg stopped the
rehearsal:
    'Nia, can I just ask – what gender are you playing?'
    'I'm a man, I'm a man,' she cried desperately.
    'Then why are you wearing heels?'
    'It's a long story – it's my quick change – it won't be like this on
the night.'
    'And what's that weapon you're carrying?'
    'A butter churn.'
    'A butter churn?'
    'Yes – I'm going to churn the enemy to death. It's the only thing
that she – he – *my soldier* – could find on the farm to bring along.'
    'Right,' said Greg with a sigh; 'Carry on.'

Afternoon. As we were preparing for the run, I saw a small, white-
haired figure enter the room.
    'Oh no,' I muttered; 'God is watching the run.'
    Misunderstanding, Jonny Glynn said, 'Only if you're a believer.'
    'Unfortunately, in this case I *am*,' I replied, watching Ciss Berry

take a seat next to Greg. She has represented the spirit of the RSC ever since I joined the company thirty-two years ago. I wondered why Greg hadn't warned me she was coming. Probably just as well. It would've added to my anxiety.

In the event, the run went splendidly. *Part I* is a magnificent piece of machinery, with every part of it perfectly constructed and working together like a dream; it's a Rolls-Royce of a play. All you have to do is go on the journey.

I felt sufficiently relaxed to watch the other half of the play – the rebels' story – and was struck by Trevor White's Hotspur. It's a very original reading of the role: a boy-man with a wild, gleeful appetite for danger. I'm full of admiration when I see one of Shakespeare's great roles fresh-minted: admiration for the actor in imagining it anew, and admiration for Shakespeare in allowing such endless reinterpretation.

Seeing Trevor's performance helped me understand something about the different nature of the two plays. Hotspur is one of the most charismatic figures in all of Shakespeare. But he's dead by the time of *Part II*, and now the rebels are led by the Archbishop of York. Keith Osborn is playing him with great fervour, turning 'insurrection to religion', but the character is simply no match for Hotspur. So the rebel scenes are less exciting. Which isn't great for a *sequel*. And hence our struggle with it.

Although I felt good after this afternoon's run, I tried to avoid speaking to Ciss directly – better to get her opinion filtered through Greg. But then I saw her heading towards me on her walking stick, and bolted over to save her the effort.

'That was great, darling,' she said quietly. Ciss is the least theatrical of people, yet she does call you 'darling' (it just means 'my dear') and often describes things as 'great' (it just means 'okay').

Unsure whether she was referring to the whole show or my performance, I floundered: 'Good... yes... and isn't it the most outrageous thing Shakespeare ever wrote?'

'What?'

'Falstaff.'

'Mm. But dark too.'

'Yes, yes' – *hadn't I played the dark side?* – 'That's what I mean by outrageous.'

She thought for a moment, then said, 'None of you were really finding the language today – you had other things on your minds. But when you do, and when he, Falstaff, when his thoughts are moving faster, it'll be lovely.'

This is Ciss's first principle: the speed and lightness of the text. I've always suspected that she feels *acting* gets in the way. Particularly character acting, where the mannerisms of a different voice might lead to a different rhythm of speech. Falstaff's posh drawl does slow down some of his lines. It's right for him, but maybe isn't the ideal way of speaking Shakespeare.

So – I don't think I really got God's approval today.

But I will take her note: *think* faster.

It corresponds to something I feel about my performance. It needs to be more effortless.

Evening. Dinner in The Dirty Duck – to mark our last night of freedom. Father Alex Austin was there and came to say hello. He's the priest at Stratford's Catholic Church, St Gregory's, and has a long history with the Doran family. He was a novice monk at Douai Abbey in Berkshire when Greg's uncle, another Greg, was the Abbot, and many years later, in 2010, he conducted the funeral service for Greg's dad. Although Greg is a lapsed Catholic ('I never lapsed, I jumped!' he likes to say), Father Alex has shrewdly perceived a strong strain of Catholicism in his work. And indeed *Henry IV Part I* begins with that Latin motet, to bolster the King's dream of going on crusade to Jerusalem. (By chance, Paul Englishby went to the same Catholic College in Preston as Greg did.) Tonight, we told Father Alex about the new house we'll soon be getting – it's not far from his church. He said mischievously, 'I'll pop over and give it a blessing on the quiet.'

Greg laughed. 'Do – at this point in time all blessings are welcome!'

5. Fat Knight – First Night

There's a new countdown: thirty-three days to the opening on the 16th April, when we'll perform both plays to the press.

Today's *Times* has a joint interview with Greg and me, alongside a piece about power couples in the arts. We're listed as number one.

'No pressure then,' says Greg, as he shows me the article on his iPad. But I'm too preoccupied to take proper notice. I'm leaning over the bathroom sink, peering into the mirror, armed with a beard-trimmer and razor. This is an experiment which I've been planning for weeks, and saved for this morning. My beard, which has grown very full indeed, naturally creeps up towards my cheekbones, and this creates a kind of shadow, a flattering illusion, which makes my face look slimmer than it is. To achieve the opposite effect, I remove this hair, and take my beard-line further over towards my ears and lower down towards my chin, showing as much flesh as possible. The result is everything I hoped for. I have a much broader, bigger face – a fat face.

I hurry to the theatre, to my dressing room, eager to continue this magic trick, this special disguise, this Jekyll-and-Hyde game. It's the moment when the character actor's fantasy turns into reality. There's a new make-up product on the market called Skin Illustrator, created during the filming of *Pirates of the Caribbean*, when they needed something that wouldn't come off with water; they had the sea to contend with, I have sweat. The beard-whitener has a slight stiffening agent, so as I apply it, I also use it to widen my beard. The false eyebrows further widen my face. The wig widens my whole head. And with reddish colours for booze-bruising and age-puffiness, I widen my nose and my lips. It's all about horizontal lines, everything going to either side.

Now into the body suit, and the costume over it. The shirt has been artfully dyed by the wardrobe department, with perspiration patches outlining the moobs, and food stains on the belly. A shabby waistcoat, enormous trousers, and gouty old boots. A worn baldrick and belt helps to show off the swell of the torso and waist. And finally, the pièce de résistance: that great, long, leather, cowboy-ish coat.

There's a full-length mirror on the back of my dressing-room door. Falstaff stands before me. I catch my breath. I've never been completely sure, till now, that I could achieve this image.

I try saying a few lines, watching myself. And now it strikes me that two different instincts have mixed together fruitfully. In rehearsals, Falstaff has been emerging as more and more posh, while in costume fittings I've wanted him to look as dilapidated as possible. The result: a grand tramp. I wouldn't have been able to articulate this, as an interpretation of the role, but my subconscious has, and I like the conflict that I'm now seeing in the mirror: Falstaff's elevated sense of himself and the circumstances of his actual life. As a man, he is both a real force and a complete dreamer.

Over the last couple of hours, there's been a serious growth surge – the role coming together before my very eyes.

It's always a critical moment when you appear in your costume and make-up at the tech and everyone sees you for the first time. I know I'm on to a good thing when Simon Ash, the Production Manager, who would never normally comment on the artistic side of things, passes me backstage and says, 'You look great!'

I'm happy to report that the whole cast are looking great. Stephen BL has a clever way of keeping the design Elizabethan while using other periods to illuminate some characters: the shape of Rakehell's hat and fur-collared coat suggest a Dickensian ne'er-do-well, Bardolph's Shrewsbury helmet reminds you of a WWI Tommy. And Mistress Quickly's costume has a threadbare gentility which is just slightly clownish – it perfectly complements Paola's Felliniesque performance; she's Italian, of course, and like the characters in the Maestro's films, her Quickly belongs both to the real world and the world of fairgrounds and sideshows. [*Photo insert, page 5, Paola Dionisotti as Mistress Quickly*]

Wanting to see the rest of Stephen's work, I go out front. The stalls are like Mission Control, Houston, with work consoles and screens everywhere, for the different departments: lighting, sound, music, stage management, and one for Greg. Stephen's vast wooden set is even more ingenious than it looked on the model, and more atmospheric, with hazy shafts of light filtering through the wattle slats (Tim Mitchell and Stephen have worked together so much, they have a total symbiosis), and it blends into the auditorium itself, so that the whole theatre has become the world of the play.

The look of it all sends a charge of excitement through the whole company. Sean Chapman says, 'It makes you just want to give this to an audience. It makes you put all your own fear aside, and just say, "Here, have this!"'

The long stop-start nature of a tech is hard-going for a man weighed down with a body suit. I keep needing to sit. But discover an odd problem. I can't easily aim myself into a chair. It's as if the human bum has its own sensory device, and mine has been foiled by all the padding.

And I haven't yet tried going for a pee. With all the layers – the costume, the body suit, my own underwear – and a route of flies, flaps and fastenings, I'm not at all convinced that I'll be able to find my willy. The stuff of trauma. Even if you haven't just played Sigmund Freud. So I wait until the meal breaks, when I'm back in my own clothes.

Greg is renowned for the speed of his techs, and gets a lot of Brownie points from the technical staff. (Some other directors use techs to rehearse the scenes.) By the evening session we're well into the tavern scene, which finishes the first half. But today's workload has been tiring, and it starts to show.

We've just done the section about 'three misbegotten knaves in Kendal green', when Greg stops the action:

'Tony, you can't say that.'

'What?'

'You just said "knaves in Kensal Green" – that's a stop on the Northern Line.'

'Did I? Sorry. It's very late.'

Laughter from those assembled, topped by Paola:

'At least he didn't say Golders Green.'

Saturday 15 March

Yesterday Stephen BL and Head Wiggy Sandra Smith decided that my wig and beard were too white; apparently the lighting made it look like I just had a fuzzy glow round my face. So today the wig has some darker streaks, the eyebrows are darker too – better, fiercer – and I've let some of my own beard colour show through.

More dramatically, Trevor's hair has been dyed white-blond. He looks like a cross between Klaus Kinski and (when in the chain-mail armour) Max von Sydow in *The Seventh Seal*. There's a vaguely Nazi look to him now as well, which is appropriate for a Hotspur who's inflamed with war-fever.

In the lunch break, Greg and I ate sandwiches in my dressing room, which boasts a view of the Avon that would do any five-star hotel proud. What other theatre in the world has this aspect? It was a sunny Saturday afternoon, people were boating on the river or strolling on the banks, and Joshua Bell was playing his violin beautifully on my CD machine. There was a sense of peace and happiness, which isn't what the middle of techs normally feel like.

Greg said, 'Quite a lot of our life has been by this river.'

For the rest of the day, we tech'd Acts Three and Four. I carry a piece of paper in my costume, making notes of everything: my entrances and exits, the 101 adjustments to what we were doing in rehearsals. It's all so unfamiliar, even the backstage routes and areas (this is my first time in the main theatre since it was rebuilt), but the feeling *will* pass...

Sunday 16 March

It's most unusual to have a day off during a tech, and most welcome.

Monday 17 March

All day spent teching the battle scenes. Which meant all day in the armour. And it's heavy. Combined with the body suit, it was too much. I could feel the strain on my back. But it was just a case of getting through it. I'll never have to wear the armour for as long again.

Trevor White as Hotspur

Evening. First dress rehearsal of *Part I*. The job was just to remember everything – with the help of the crib notes in my pocket. It all went fairly smoothly. At one point the truck stopped moving – the raised platform which brings on different sets – but this turned out to be operator error which is much better than machine error. An operator will be more mindful in the future. A machine has a mind of its own.

I was pleased by the amount of rest breaks that Falstaff gets – many more than the other Shakespeare biggies that I've played.

But the best news was this: in the interval, I finally decided to try having a pee while wearing all the gear, and I *did* find my willy. Relief in every sense.

Tuesday 18 March

The sun was shining, so, before work, we took our first river walk into the countryside. The fields had just been turned – great expanses of rich, dark soil in glistening chunks and slabs. The trees were still bare, but there were buds on every branch, about to open. Any moment it'll be spring.

Afternoon. Second dress rehearsal of *Part I*. A chance to *get to know* the show better. A minor emergency: my wig shifted when Alex grabbed the cushion/crown from my head in the 'play within the play'. Good for it to happen now, rather than in performance. The solution is for me to take the cushion off myself.

Evening. First preview of *Part I*. I'm normally in a state of shock and disbelief at this point. What, the show is no longer ours – a crowd of *strangers* are going to come and watch it?! But not tonight. Falstaff has to have a strong relationship with the audience. I'm keen to know what that'll be like.

(As today's workload accelerated, I could only make brief notes in this diary.)

Addressing the company beforehand, Greg told us two things:

• Preview audiences at the RSC are often overgenerous and wildly appreciative.
• We'll get some laughs we weren't expecting, and not get others that we were.

He was right about the second point, but not the first.

The audience was hard work, not generous at all, barely appreciative.

Were they just a 'bad' audience (i.e. quiet, flat, slow to respond) or was it us?

They took a long, long time to warm up to Falstaff. In fact, it wasn't till my very last scene ('Embowelled?') that they were thoroughly enjoying him.

Was it them or me?

I've got to admit the evening was a struggle, a disappointment. Had to give myself pep talk after pep talk.

We've always said that we didn't want Falstaff just to be a comic role, that we wanted him to be complex and dark too.

Well, that seems to have been achieved.

But it didn't feel right.

The rest of the cast thought differently. They were excited by the fact that there were cheers at the curtain call (I was indifferent by then), and Greg was pleased too.

Back at Avonside, ignoring our house rule – *no talk about work* – I asked, 'Have we taken a completely wrong turn with Falstaff?'

He replied, 'Absolutely not.'

Wednesday 19 March

I awoke feeling worried and whacked (yesterday was effectively a two-show day).

We did notes sitting in a circle in the Ashcroft Room from 12 to 1.30, then lunch, then working notes on stage with full technical back-up.

Afterwards, Greg came to my dressing room – to discuss how I should approach tonight's show. He said, 'Laughter cannot be the barometer of your performance.' He was right. Last night was a classic example of the danger of rehearsal-room laughs. Every time one *didn't* come, I felt a tiny sense of failure. These accumulated during the evening until I was seriously concerned by the end, seriously doubting my whole interpretation of Falstaff.

Dear God, I've been an actor for four decades, and I'm still falling for that one: *rehearsal-room laughs.*

In the event, tonight's audience was much warmer: they *got* the nature of the play right from the start, they *got* Falstaff, and there were more laughs than there had ever been in rehearsals.

So – last night we simply had a 'bad' audience. During a run, you can recognise these instantly, but at a first preview you have nothing to judge them by.

Thursday 20 March

The production photos have arrived. A camera is somehow more objective than a mirror, so this is when you get to see your character properly for the first time. I was pleased. The image we've devised for Falstaff really has worked. Who'd have thought I could be so happy to look so fat?

If you keep drying or fluffing on the same speech, it's necessary to find out why. My worst pitfall has been the soliloquy in the scarecrow-army scene. Looking at the lines again, I suddenly detected one of the problems. My script was the same one I've had since I accepted this job. The page was covered in pencil and pen scribbles: suggested cuts I'd marked out in New Zealand, real cuts we'd made later, a list of word meanings, and other notes. I've always said that the layout of a text helps in learning it. Well, the layout here was a complete mess.

Sitting at my make-up table, I wrote out a clean version.

But will this solve it?

The truth is I'm worried about the scene itself. Firstly, there's that procession of desperate souls staggering across the stage behind me. I try not to look at them, but when I do catch a glimpse, I wish my fellow actors were doing *less*. The characterisations are still quite extreme, quite eye-catching. And the lighting isn't as dim as I expected. Sometimes the audience become mesmerised by the trail of figures, and start giggling.

Secondly, I'm also struggling with a lot of props. Falstaff has a little wooden cart with a fold-out stool and a picnic hamper. As he talks about his wretched soldiers, he brings out a roast chicken and prepares to feast. We're using a real one, because I'm supposed to eat some. The props department half-cut the legs so that they're easier to tear off. But in last night's show, when I tried to lift the chicken, the whole thing just disintegrated.

'This is too much,' I said to Greg afterwards; 'I've got the Ministry of Funny Walks behind me, and an exploding chicken in my hands!'

We resolved to use a prop chicken – I never get a chance to eat it anyway.

The irony is that people who've seen the dress rehearsals and previews say this is one of the most effective scenes. A chilling image of war. A fat man having a picnic while his troops march away to become cannon fodder.

All of this is Greg's invention. I've contributed no ideas at all, and am just doing what my director tells me to. Which isn't the way we normally work. It's an odd thought, but is that why I'm not comfortable with it yet...?

In the surreal nature of theatre, characters from the *Henries* intermingle with those from *Wolf Hall/Bring Up the Bodies* in the dressing-room corridors. So Falstaff had a chat with Henry VIII today, before their respective shows. I congratulated him – Nat Parker – on the phenomenal success they're having in the Swan. Being an old cynic, I remarked that these only happen a couple of times in a career, so I urged him to enjoy it. There was no need. He said the experience had restored his passion for stage acting. We were talking during their break between matinee and evening performances, and he said he couldn't wait to get out there again. Good God, that is true love. I haven't felt that way on a matinee day for a very long time.

Third preview. A dream audience. The show flew, I flew. (Lines perfect in the scarecrow-army scene.) Tonight I could be forgiven for believing again that we've got a success.

Friday 21 March

I love this process of using the previews to refine, adjust, and improve the show. The audience has become part of the creative team: they're teaching us what works and what doesn't. And inspiring us to new things.

Today we made a small but exciting alteration to the section where Hal puts Falstaff in command of a company of foot soldiers. I've been accepting the document grumpily, muttering the next line:

'Well, God be thanked for these rebels, they offend none but the virtuous. I laud them, I praise them.' But we've become aware of a little shockwave going through the audience, and realised that the statement is more scandalous than we thought: it's like declaring yourself to be a Nazi sympathiser in wartime Britain. So now I'm saying it boldly, defiantly, and *not* accepting the document. Hal has to force it into my hands, shouting: 'The land is burning!' Good stuff: Falstaff at his most subversive, and Hal starting to morph into Henry V.

As part of this afternoon's work, Greg also choreographed a proper curtain call (up until now, we've just been tumbling on in one big free-for-all), and then, like at the end of each of these sessions, he asked us to summarise the main changes we're putting in this evening. Otherwise, these can surprise you in performance, trip you up.

Ciss sits at the back during these afternoon sessions. She sees all the previews and even came to the tech. It's a marvellous thing. While other people of her age (eighty-eight) would be going to their bridge club or game of bowls, she is simply doing what she's always done: being at the RSC. The other day she was telling me that her eyesight is increasingly poor ('It's fucking embarrassing, darling'), but when she's hearing a piece of Shakespeare her whole being lights up, including her eyes. She listens to language as if it's music. [*Photo insert, page 6, Ciss Listening*]

Tonight's audience was as good as last night's. Falstaff was getting so many laughs that I now began to worry whether the darker side of my characterisation was coming across. When I ran on for my solo bow at the curtain call, the noise was quite something to hear, quite primal – like I'd done a good kill at the Colosseum.

Line-wise, they were pretty good – except for in the 'Honour' speech, when I rearranged them a bit.

Afterwards in my dressing room, Greg was buzzing about the show. Then he said, 'And I know you threw yourself in the "Honour" speech, but no one noticed – Tim Mitchell thought it was particularly good.'

'I didn't throw myself,' I answered sharply; 'I made a mistake, but I recovered well.'

'You did.'

'So I didn't throw myself. Sorry if it threw you.'

It was a funny moment between us. Each time I stumble on the lines (which is very seldom, really), he must get a tiny fright.

Saturday 22 March

In brief moments of relaxation – usually on the loo – I'm reading a book of essays on Shakespeare by Peter Brook, *The Quality of Mercy*. He's very eloquent. For example, here he is on the ten-beat rhythm of the iambic pentameter:

'True thought has a feeling, and it is the feeling that has a music in its flow. Shakespeare, in the passionate velocity of finding words for the formless tumult within him, never counted from one to ten. This was a deep part of his consciousness, and so in his mature writing, when the pressure of feeling was stronger than correctness, he violated his own rules.'

I remember that very thing from when we did *The Winter's Tale* (one of the late plays) – the sense that Shakespeare had become a master jazz musician, able to improvise around the beat while keeping the melody going.

One of the curious truths about theatre is that Saturday-night audiences are usually 'bad'. Maybe because they've paid more for their tickets and come with an attitude: *this better be worth it.* Anyway, it was certainly the case with this evening's crowd, but it didn't matter. The show, and our characters, were soaked into us now, nicely marinated, and performing this great play was simply a pleasure.

Afterwards, over supper in The Dirty Duck, and then walking back to Avonside – it was a cold, dark night – we had an inspiring talk about Falstaff:

I was saying what a phenomenal creation he is. We know that Shakespeare writes villains well – Iago, Richard III – monsters who subvert the natural order, and here is someone who does the same, yet isn't a villain (just a thieving, alcoholic, unscrupulous bastard), and the audience absolutely love him.

Greg said, 'He could only have been written after the Reformation, and in the Renaissance. When God is no longer the centre of the universe – Man is. It's no longer the life to come, it's life here and now. At Shrewsbury, Falstaff says, "Give me life!" It's his battle cry, even if it means, in real battle conditions, he's a hopeless coward.'

And Greg was revelatory about Falstaff's constant claim to being young. (In *Part I*, at Gad's Hill, he says 'They hate us youth'; in *Part II*, he says to the Lord Chief Justice, 'You that are old consider not the capacities of us that are young.') I've had real difficulty with this – it simply seems silly. But Greg said, 'No – it's not mutton dressed as lamb, he has a genuinely youthful spirit. The young don't think about dying, they have no sense of mortality, they live life for the day – "*Give me life*"! Of course, reality creeps up on him in *Part II*, and he gets to fear old age more and more, but he fights against it, his subversive spirit fights on…'

As we talked, I felt reassured about an aspect of my performance, which has had a mental question mark over it: the childlike aspect. As written, the part has a narcissism that is positively infantile – he is the original *enfant terrible* – and moments of extreme, immature vulnerability (like the line Greg quoted before our double run-through: 'I would it were bedtime Hal, and all well'). But I've added to it, by needing help to lift the bottle to my mouth in the first scene, and flapping my hand at Hal when I want my horse at Gad's Hill, like a kid asking Daddy to lift him up. At these times, Falstaff is not so much Hal's surrogate father as his adopted son. This feels more valid now.

This conversation tonight was a wonderful thing, a thoroughly Stratford thing, when the great themes of the great plays are chewed over and digested along with a meal in The Duck and a stroll back to your digs in the writer's home town.

Sunday 23 March

Dead man walking. That's me today.

Monday 24 March

Twenty-three days to the opening.

'Let's see how it comes out of its box.'

This is how Greg talked about revisiting *Part II* today. We were back in the Michel Saint-Denis rehearsal room – how strange, yet reassuring – working through the play, scene by scene.

Some bits were refreshed by the break, and some were unfamiliar. Nia said that suddenly playing Doll again was 'like bumping into an old, very needy friend.' But other bits were positively enriched by the experience of performing *Part I* to an audience.

Both Alex and I remarked on how we felt we *owned* our characters more than whenever last we were in this room. And the impact of Hal's rejection of Falstaff was a hundredfold – having played the *Part I* tavern scene, where Falstaff jokes again and again about banishment, leading to one of the most famous moments in the play:

FALSTAFF: ...Banish plump Jack and banish all the world.

HAL: I do, I will.

The main sensation in today's work was of delight. The same characters, but in different situations. It was like being in a posh soap – a soap written by Shakespeare.

Oliver Ford Davies was back with us today, and he had a curious little gift for me: he said he had been concerned about the sound of one of my lines, had checked various editions, and had a suggestion.

The line was in the alcohol speech, when Falstaff talks about it making the brain 'apprehensive, quick, forgetive'.

I've been saying, 'forget-tive' (as in 'forget'). Olly thought it might be 'forge-i-tive' (as in 'forge'). Which makes sense, since the word means 'inventive', and the implication of 'forgetting' was not helpful.

But it's going to be hard to relearn the pronunciation of something I've been saying wrong for months. I immediately stick up notices on the mirrors in my dressing room and in our Avonside bathroom, and start repeating the new version like a mantra. '*Forge-i-tive.*'

Time to forget 'forget-tive', and forge ahead with '*forge-i-tive*'.

Tuesday 25 March

We are, bizarrely, back in a tech.

And I'm marvelling again at how Stephen BL's supremely simple set keeps providing strong new images for every new scene. It's done with minimal furniture and maximum atmosphere (i.e. Tim's lighting). Greg has placed Act Two, Scene Two in the changing room of tennis courts (there's a line about the 'tennis-court keeper', and of course tennis balls will feature prominently in *Henry V*), and this is created just with a bench and a stool. Alex and Sam Marks (Poins) enter with tennis rackets, and proceed to change out of their sweaty sport shirts.

Today, when the chaps are bare-chested, some of the actresses are watching from the stalls, and begin wolf-whistling. One of them calls out, 'Thank you, Greg Doran!' If this had been the other way round – males making lustful noises about females stripping – there would be outrage. There's liberation for you!

In *Part II*, Falstaff's new look, as he now plays at being the 'Hero of Shrewsbury', is perfect: minimalist and a bit tacky. A few feathers in his hat, a red sash across his torso, and a little medal which looks like it came out of a Christmas cracker. This is suitably upstaged by Simon Thorp's costume as the LCJ: fine black and scarlet robes, and a *real* chain of office.

News comes that the actor Jeffrey Dench has died. A real stalwart of the RSC. Greg stops the tech, asks everyone to gather in the auditorium – cast and crew – and does a tribute to Jeffrey. Then says, 'An actor doesn't want a minute's silence – let's give him a round of applause!' Later, Jeffrey's sister, Judi, sends a message thanking Greg for the gesture.

Simon Thorp
as L. C. J.

Wednesday 26 March

Tech'd the alcohol speech. As I exited down the stage-right vom, I saw Ciss Berry sitting on one of the aisles. Muttered to her, 'That's not one for the AA.'

(She's completely open about her time as an alcoholic – in her youth.)

She replied in that way of hers, mixing the streetwise and the theatrical: 'Too fucking right, darling!'

She had a good note for me. Asked, 'Who pays Falstaff?'

I replied, 'Well, when he's on active service, like now, the State does.'

'Exactly. There's that pressure on him.'

Realised I was playing the exchange with Prince John too lightly. The knight Coleville has surrendered to Falstaff – surprisingly – and Falstaff wants the Prince to 'let it be booked with this day's deeds'; he wants the credit, the reward. Like what Hal did at Shrewsbury: backing the absurd story that Falstaff killed Hotspur. But John is a very different, much colder character (excellently played by Elliot Barnes-Worrell), and resists all Falstaff's attempts at humour and banter.

Ciss was reminding me that the stakes are higher.

In playing Falstaff, the constant danger is just being fatuous. *The fat knight isn't fatuous.*

Thursday 27 March

First dress rehearsal of *Part II*. I felt good. Last Saturday night's conversation about Falstaff's 'youth' has transformed things. In that troublesome early scene with the Lord Chief Justice, the lines about 'we that are young' are no longer just hot air, but deeply felt. Yet so is the moment when Falstaff says 'I am old' to Doll Tearsheet a few scenes later. Connecting these two points is a strong thing to play. And the theme of ageing builds through the Shallow scene – 'the days that we have seen' – and culminates in Hal's rejection of Falstaff: 'I know thee not, old man.' We have borrowed Ralph Richardson's version of this climactic moment (as reported by Kenneth Tynan): I keep my back to the audience throughout Hal's speech, and then only turn out front when he's gone. Falstaff is poleaxed, but trying to talk, trying to work out what's happened. 'Look you, he must seem thus to the world,' he says of his best buddy, now King Henry V, and twice insists: 'I *shall* be sent for.'

Friday 28 March

Slept for ten hours! Felt excited about tonight. The audience will teach us...

First preview of *Part II*. Braced myself for no laughs, but there were lots (maybe ongoing affection for Falstaff from people who've seen *Part I*), even in the alcohol speech: I said the line about how, if I had a thousand sons, the first thing I'd teach them is to 'addict themselves to sack' and there was a roar of laughter. Extraordinary. They were celebrating the idea of a father turning his children into alcoholics. There's proof of how far Shakespeare dares to take the charm factor of this character. And of course the Gloucestershire scene, with Shallow/Silence, and then the group of recruits, caused a big comic storm.

But the play itself... it's a strange beast...

Saturday 29 March

Tonight, with a very warm audience, the show felt as strong as *Part I*. A good way to end the week.

Afterwards, Greg emailed some small cuts to the actors. Which gives us tomorrow to absorb and learn them. The rule is that if you passionately want to keep a condemned line, you can do so, as long as you sacrifice another of your own lines in exchange. That way we still reduce the running time, which is too long.

Sunday 30 March

We were coming to the end of our morning stroll, approaching the church, when suddenly a roe deer – an adult, quite big – scrambled out of the water and onto the Dell, charged this way and that, then bolted across the Avonbank Gardens. A moment later we saw it swimming across the river, only to turn round, climb onto this bank again, and hurtle back towards us. Where had it come from, where

The Gloucestershire Recruits : Mouldy (Simon Yadoo), Bullcalf (Youssef Kerkour), Wart (Leigh Quinn), Shadow (Jonny Glynn), Feeble (Nick Gerard-Martin)

was it trying to go? We glanced at all the dogs out on their walks. Would they attack it? But the blind panic of a wild animal creates such a force field that the dogs were as frozen as their owners. Every living witness was just holding its breath.

As we left the gardens, I saw a man phoning the police on his mobile. But I don't know what happened to the poor deer.

Felt haunted by it all day.

Panic turning into force.

A bit like getting on a show.

Monday 31 March

Having rehearsed the new cuts this afternoon, we put them into tonight's performance, and it was eight minutes shorter. Which was good. The same could not be said for tonight's audience – they were quiet and flat – and the weaknesses of *Part II* felt exposed again.

I'm like a yo-yo on this.

Many people think *Part II* is the inferior play. I've thought so myself in the past. (Richard Eyre's TV film proved otherwise, but it doesn't strictly count; firstly, the text was so reduced, and secondly, Jeremy Irons himself admitted that he couldn't have done the same performance onstage.)

Now that we're actually doing both plays, I don't want to believe that *Part II* is going to let us down, and turn this epic experience into a broken-backed affair.

'Will fortune never come with both hands full?' asks the King in Act Four, Scene Two.

I've got my hopes on hold at the moment.

Tuesday 1 April

It's April Fool's Day, and I guess the joke is that we've got just sixteen days till the opening.

Wednesday 2 April

Today was good. A series of things made me happy.

There's a corridor on the ground floor of the backstage area, between the door to the stairs and the door to the stage, where a constant low noise is heard. Probably just to do with the air-conditioning or plumbing system, but stopping in there this morning, a different alternative occurred to me: it was like the sound of distant applause. It's as if, when they were rebuilding the theatre, rearranging its spaces and its routes, a pocket of air got trapped here, and then, when everything had settled down again, this most unexpected thing was released. Everyone talks about theatres having ghosts in the walls; they mean actors, but why not audiences too – the ghost of an audience? At the end of some show, some time in the RSC's history, when the people had enjoyed themselves, and clapped loud and long... and it's continued to echo in this one passageway.

I was still smiling at the thought, when I walked into my dressing room, opened the big window, and witnessed an astonishing specta-cle on the river. A flock of swans came in to land on the water, then took off again, and repeated the exercise. Some of them were last year's cygnets – almost fully grown, but with mottled feathers – so maybe the parents were giving them flying lessons, using this straight stretch of the Avon as their runway. When swans prepare to fly, they gallop along the surface, beating their wings on it, making a special sound – Greg calls it 'an applause of swans'. It was breathtaking. I stood on my balcony, unable to believe that this was my place of work and yet a natural wonder was happening right here before my eyes.

Glad to report that tonight's show added to the day's delights. A wonderful audience, restoring my faith in *Part II*. Despite Greg's much-repeated note to us this afternoon – 'Laughter is not the barometer of this show' – there was plenty of it, culminating in an extraordinary event in my speech at the end of the Gloucestershire scene. Falstaff is telling the audience about Shallow's wild youth, and being indiscreet about his sex life. I began the line, 'When he was naked...' but could get no further because a lone woman in the stage-right stalls began to giggle loudly. I turned to look at her. The audience guffawed. She bent forward, clutching herself. I pointed at her with my stick. A bigger guffaw. I walked over to her. The house shook. I carried on with the speech, and got to the line which has a vulgar double-meaning for a modern audience: 'He came ever in the rearward of the fashion.' As usual, people reacted with uncertainty – *did Shakespeare write that?* – but I had only to point to the woman again to ignite another explosion. I thought:

Blimey, I'm doing stand-up. With Shakespeare.

Greg was grinning broadly when he came to my dressing room afterwards. I said, 'Just call me Billy Connolly.'

Of course it was a happy accident, and is unlikely to happen again. On the other hand, there's a tradition of Falstaff being played by comics – beginning with Will Kemp (probably) and going through to George Robey – and those performers would've used all Falstaff's soliloquies to interact with the audience much more than I've been doing, or *can* do. But if I did possess those skills, would I want to use them? It's an intriguing point. If Falstaff plays with the audience like those stand-up people do, with their own personalities on show instead of his, would you still care about him as a man? Falstaff – character or clown? That is the question. I know what my answer is.

Thursday 3 April

Part I is back on tonight.

This morning I did all my lines, and this afternoon we had a company line-run, which became a walk-though – it was good to be reminded of the geography of scenes as well as their content.

But there was an emergency.

A fearsome bug, a cough/cold, has been sweeping through the company, affecting many people, though not me (which is a miracle, since I'm very susceptible to these things). Alex is the latest victim. The news gave me a jolt. Over the weeks, Alex and I have developed an onstage chemistry which is worth its weight in gold. This only happens with certain actors, and you thank God if they're part of a crucial relationship in a play, like a marriage (I struck lucky with Debbie Findlay in *Stanley* and Harriet Walter in *Macbeth*) or something like the Falstaff/Hal friendship.

In order for Alex to do tonight's show, his understudy did this afternoon's run: Sam Marks, who plays Poins. Today he did both Hal and Poins, often together in the same scene. Word perfect, very impressive.

Alex got through the show, and the whole thing was in good shape. I had a slight sense of being one step behind the action, and indeed was late on for the Battle of Shrewsbury. (But at least that was in character.)

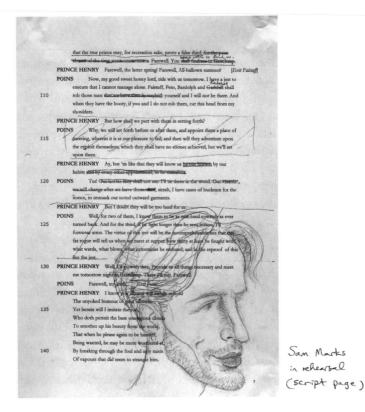

Sam Marks in rehearsal (script page)

Saturday 5 April

First time that we performed the two plays together, matinee and evening.

The task seemed so huge that there was no place for nerves.

In the event, it was an extraordinary day, when we and the audience (those who saw both shows) went on a six-hour journey through one of Shakespeare's great creations.

I was struck by how *Part II benefited* from *Part I*. I felt I was in a kind of sitcom. As soon as I came on in *Part II* I was getting what I call free laughs – not for specific lines, but just for being the same character that they'd enjoyed in *Part I*. The same was true for Mistress Quickly, Bardolph and others. It was heart-warming. And it helped disguise the true nature of *Part II*, which is sluggish and uneven – especially in comparison to the velocity of *Part I* – but the emotional power of *Part II* was suddenly all the greater for the whole story being told. Especially in terms of what happens to Falstaff and Hal. I was reminded of Jim Shapiro saying that Eastcheap is a green world, a dreamworld. This afternoon's matinee began with Falstaff and Hal waking up in a bawdy house, engaged in a terrific relationship – playful and combative – and this evening's performance ended with Hal banishing Falstaff, saying, 'I have long dreamed of such a kind of man... but being awake, I do despise my dream.' The savagery and sadness of that was very raw today, very upsetting. But the *necessity* of it was also clear: if Hal is to be a good ruler, he must get rid of the Lord of Misrule.

The long day ended with loud applause and cheers at the curtain call – so much so that we had to go back for more.

I lived in my dressing room for twelve hours today (11 a.m. to 11 p.m.) – the make-up and costume takes ages to put on and take off – which is much longer than the rest of the company. When I moaned to Greg about this, he reminded me that it was my choice. Quite right. It's another aspect of being a character actor.

When I was finally leaving the stage door, I found two Americans waiting for autographs. One said, 'Falstaff is such a great part – do you feel very lucky to have got it?' I was so exhausted I forgot to be polite, and answered, 'No, but he feels very lucky to have got me.'

Sunday 6 April

I wake feeling tired. That keeps happening. I'm running on empty.

Did my Sunday phone calls to South Africa: Randall and Verne. Our mother believed in spiritualism, and we were all sceptical about it. Today I said to them, 'Mom would be proud of you – you're talking to the dead.'

In the pursuit of energy and sugar-rushes, I'm eating everything I normally avoid – chips, chocs, cakes – yet I'm losing weight. It's the body suit, and the amount that I sweat; Rachel Seal, who puts on my wig, says I've got my own personal climate. I drink gallons of coconut water during the show, to combat dehydration, but I'm worried about the effect of weight-loss on my face. Having successfully made it look fat, I don't want any cheekbones appearing!

This is crazy. I spend my life wanting to be thinner, and now I can't control it. I've inadvertently discovered something called The Falstaff Diet.

Was telling Tony Byrne about it backstage the other day, and he suggested that the RSC should market it – sell it in the front-of-house shop. It would come as a kit: a blow-up body suit (like a love doll) and the text of both plays. The would-be dieter has to learn all Falstaff's lines, then speak them aloud in a pressurised situation – in front of neighbours, or anywhere public – while wearing the body suit. Guaranteed: the pounds will drop off you!

The one bit of good news is that my back is fine: in fact, better than it's been in years. Can it be that the burden of carrying the body suit, plus the armour in the battle scenes, is serving to *strengthen* my muscles?

Monday 7 April

This morning Greg drove to Highgrove with Catherine Mallyon for a routine catch-up with RSC President, HRH.

Meanwhile, I set about an important task: doing the sketch that I'll have printed up as my first-night cards. I've been trying to ignore the big event, even claiming that I'm not sure exactly when it is, but the time for those games is over. It's next Wednesday, the 16th; nine days away. My cartoon is based on Falstaff's line, 'Turk Gregory never did such deeds in arms as I have done today', and shows me as the Fat Knight and Greg wearing a turban. I didn't intend it, but Falstaff's look is rather lusty...

Cartoon for 1st Night card

This afternoon we did some more cuts to *Part II* and it was five minutes shorter this evening. But on its own again, without *Part I*, it was its old self: half good, half not. Greg was feeling frustrated by it at the end, and perhaps because of tiredness – the Highgrove drive was one and a half hours each way – brought his gloom back to Avonside.

'Cheer up,' I said; 'You're frightening me.'

He said, 'Well, if you want to live with a director, you're going to see the reality.'

Trouble is, I've lived with this particular director for twenty-seven years, and I've never seen him so uncertain before an opening. (Though only about *Part II*.)

Tuesday 8 April

No energy for anything. Sat gazing at the river, which was sunlit and calming. Thought that if later someone asks what I did this morning, I'll say, 'I looked at the river,' and it will not have been an unimportant thing, or a waste of time.

God, I'm going to miss Avonside. Much as I'm looking forward to the new house... [*Photo insert, page 7, 'G&T at Avonside'*]

Mind you, if I'm knackered, what about everyone else? Just two examples. Jenny Kirby is giving a heartfelt (and sexy) performance as Lady Percy, but also has to play a tavern lass and a scarecrow soldier – thankless but tiring work – and understudy Doll. Rob Gilbert does a strong double as Mortimer and Coleville, plays another scarecrow soldier, a drawer, a carrier, a groom, and understudies Hotspur, which means not only learning all the lines, but that big, difficult fight with Hal. There are understudy rehearsals all the time (taken by Owen Horsley), alongside Greg's calls. The company is being worked to its limits. Being at the RSC is not for sissies.

This evening's audience – for *Part I* – was probably the best we've had: packed to the rafters and wild with enthusiasm. On occasions like this I always say that the show flew, I flew – but tonight it was almost true. At one point I felt so exhilarated that I had a sort of out-of-body experience: it was as though I lifted out of myself, and saw this enormous theatre, filled with this joyful crowd, and there in the middle of it – there I was playing Falstaff. Now *that* wasn't written into my destiny. And all the more fucking marvellous for it!

Jenny Kirby in rehearsal (script page)

Wednesday 9 April

The day was hot and glorious. In Stratford we call this matinee weather. The sun is somehow guaranteed to shine whenever we're trapped inside a dark theatre for a whole day.

So – the marathon again: *Parts I* and *II*. When my contract was being negotiated, I'd specifically asked for more of these double-days to be scheduled during the preview period. Part of the job with Shakespeare's great roles is just learning how to *pace* yourself.

The start of this one is quite unique:

Falstaff's first entrance is from under a pile of bedding at the foot of Hal's bed. Beforehand, in pitch darkness at the back of the stage, I'm helped into a prone position by Daisy (our ASM), and then Kevin (from Props) whispers, 'All right, Tony?' I whisper back, 'Yes thanks,' and feel him place the quilts over me. I keep open a little section to breathe, then lie there waiting. I always think: *what a totally bizarre way to begin a major job of work…!*

A good sign. During today's shows, I stopped fretting about the work, and was relaxed (or tired) enough to sit back and look around me. The spectacle of backstage life…! For years I've wanted to do a big painting of it, but I simply don't know how to capture the sheer variety of activity and pace.

The setting is one of the wings on either side of the RST stage: a shadowy, blue-lit area which is locked in permanent night-time. On floor level, it is crowded with prop cupboards, prop tables, stage furniture and chairs just for sitting. But a few metres higher it becomes an empty, incredibly tall space, reaching all the way up to the flies, where pieces of set and lighting bars are suspended. The wing is populated by dozens of people dressed in three different ways: some (the actors) are in costume, many more (stage crew, stage managers, dressers and wiggies) are wearing black clothes and radio-contact equipment, and a few (those stage hands who will appear on the stage to move scenery) are in a mixture of both: rudimentary costume and radio-contact equipment.

One or two of the actors are about to enter the present scene, and stand in that poised state, that particular stillness, containing adrenalin, nerves, and a memory bank of words. Other actors are waiting for the next scene, sitting in their regular seats – it can be a plastic chair or a throne – and holding whispered conversations, or sipping at bottles of mineral water, or (if they've been at understudy rehearsals all day) catching a quick nap. Another actor has just exited, and has a quick change ahead: they run, fast but quiet, beginning to undo belts and buttons. In the quick-change room – an improvised, tent-like structure – they are set upon by dressers and wiggies, with busy hands grabbing, lifting, lowering. It can feel like being mugged. Meanwhile, other dressers and wiggies have nothing to do for now; they've brought along books, magazines, and crossword puzzles, and seek out any spill of light to see by. A stage manager is knitting, with one dutiful eye on the big colour monitor which shows the onstage action; they will *never* miss their next cue. Another stage manager is walking purposively, carrying a prop – it was deposited on stage-left during the last scene, and needs to arrive from stage-right in the next one. The stage crew have long, long waits during the performance. These days they have iPhones to alleviate the boredom, and their faces are lit by the tiny, cool glow of their screens. The Wardrobe Mistress passes, wheeling a small trolley of used costumes...

There's the sudden arrival of men in armour: actors who've being changing in their dressing rooms. They go to the sword rack and collect their weapons.

Now, abruptly, everyone is on their feet, and milling towards the entrances: actors lining up in a prescribed order, stage crew manning ropes or preparing to go onstage to clear the set. Cue lights have come on here and there in the dark, showing red. On the little black-and-white monitor the Musical Director can be seen in front of the band (they're in a separate room, high above the stage); he's wearing headphones, and holds up his fingers in a countdown: two, one, *and* – the music starts. The stage lights dim. The cue lights turn green. The wings empty. After just a few seconds, the crew returns, the stage lights brighten, the music fades, and you hear the actors beginning the new scene...

Thursday 10 April

Greg mustered his forces, and did a lot of work on *Part II* today. 'We're learning its true nature in performance,' he told the company; 'Much more than with *Part I*. That came fully formed. It's so strong, you just have to *do* it. Easy-peasy. *Part II* is a much subtler, stranger thing. But a fine thing. Maybe we've been regarding it too much as a dying fall from *Part I*. Well, a dying fall can't sustain a whole evening. It's got its own dynamic. And we're finding it, we're getting there!'

He did a good exercise with the Pistol section of the tavern scene. Asked us to do it without all the frenetic moves – just sitting in a circle of chairs, talking to one another, really connecting. Then we put the moves back in. Suddenly the scene was more febrile, more dangerous, more *important*. It ceased to be a kind of turn – which needed laughs and wasn't getting them – now it was real life in this tavern: booze-fuelled craziness. This affected the Falstaff/Doll relationship too. Nia and I began fighting more, loving more. She's so good. I can't imagine a better Doll.

Nia Gwynne as Doll

With Alex, Greg has been tracing a new route for Hal through *Part II*: finding out who he can trust. Best friend Poins? Maybe not. (In the tennis scene, Hal discovers that Poins might be trying to engineer a marriage to his sister.) Old mentor Falstaff? Not on your nelly. (In the tavern scene, Hal overhears Falstaff bad-mouthing him.) Enemy number one, the Lord Chief Justice? Yes, surprisingly. (When the King dies, LCJ swears allegiance to Hal.) Hal's journey to the crown is tenser now, more paranoid, more exciting.

For my own part, I gave myself a subtitle for tonight's show – 'The Fears and Decay of Sir John Falstaff' – and the results were surprising. Maybe they're things I've noted before, but it's different when you're out there doing it. I realised that Falstaff is besieged by danger, whether from within (his health: gout, possible pox, ageing) or from without: he's still accountable for the Gad's Hill robbery (punishment: death), and Mistress Quickly tries to get him arrested for debt, and at Gaultree Forest he has to physically confront the knight Coleville. There's new spitefulness in him: people only have to leave his company for him to start rubbishing them. Best of all – because it accords with an audience's response to *Part II* – is that he can no longer make people laugh like he did before: his humour falls flat with LCJ, Hal, and especially Prince John. And, as an alcoholic, he's no longer trying to clean up his act – his happiest speech is now a hymn to sherry-sack. He is an embittered, vulnerable old soak, trying to cover up reality with a few tired jokes. This is Falstaff in *Part II*. And this is who I played tonight. The changes to my performance were probably quite minimal, but they were vital. And felt right. As did the whole evening. When, in Act Four, Scene One, the Archbishop of York cried, 'We are all diseased', he was describing the one thing that unites this disparate play.

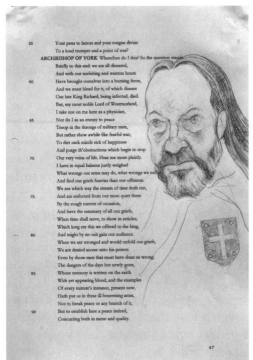

Keith Osborn as the Archbishop (script page)

We had our smallest audience so far, yet did our best show.

I hesitate to say this aloud, or even write it down, but I think we've cracked *Part II*.

Friday 11 April

A complete change of focus, thank the Lord. The Irish President, Michael D. Higgins, is in the middle of a historic visit to England. The Queen gave a state dinner in his honour at Windsor, he addressed both Houses of Parliament, and, being a poet and writer, he specially requested coming to Stratford. The RSC is hosting him here.

So this morning Greg gave him a tour of the building, which was crawling with security people, and then brought him into the main theatre for a short performance. First, three of our actors – Trevor, Sean and Tony – spoke the words of some famous Irishmen who'd been to Stratford:

Wilde, unveiling the Shakespeare Memorial that had been carved by his friend Gower in 1888, commented on Falstaff 'indulging in that eternal laughter which time has not been able to dull'.

Yeats was so moved by seeing six of the History Plays together in 1901, he wrote, 'That strange procession of kings and queens, of warring nobles, of insurgent crowds, of courtiers, and of people of the gutter, has been to me almost too visible, too audible, too full of unearthly energy.'

Shaw, when asked in 1925 to propose the toast to the Immortal Memory on Shakespeare's birthday, finally agreed to do it. He'd been declining for years, saying that since he never celebrated his own birthday, he could hardly celebrate that of 'a lesser dramatist'. He hated the architecture of the Memorial Theatre, and when it burned down the following year, he sent the Board a telegram: 'Congratulations!'

Then we performed the 'play within the play' from the tavern scene. And then Higgins came onstage – a diminutive, white-haired gent – and gave as fine a speech about language as only an Irishman could:

'The words exchanged between Ireland and England have often been part of a long and sometimes tortured exchange… Here in this place, sacred to the English language and its many glories, it would be inauthentic and foolish to gloss over the truth, since at the heart of language there is and must be a passion for truth. Today I want to acknowledge a great truth: the English language that we share, if it was once the enforced language of conquest, it is today the very language in which we have now come to delight in one another.'

I found the whole event rather stirring – to be reminded that our theatre is a place of pilgrimage, and not just, as it sometimes seems to us, an unforgiving workplace.

The media were here in force today, and as they were being guided round, one of our press officers showed me a bizarre piece from this morning's *Daily Telegraph*, in a column called 'Mandrake'. It claims that I visited Clarence House to discuss Falstaff with Prince Charles. Is this a form of Chinese whispers following Greg's trip to High-grove on Monday? Anyway, it's one of those things that, because it's in print, will now seem like truth, and some members of the audience will watch my performance wondering which bits were suggested by HRH.

Saturday 12 April

There are times when the demands of this giant part – the mental pressure plus the physical discomfort – start to feel overwhelming. My chief enemy is exhaustion. This I morning took two vitamin C tablets, one Berocca, drank several cups of coffee, and at the end of my shower turned the temperature to cold for thirty seconds. This is the equivalent of jumping off Big Rock on Saunders Beach back at home in Sea Point. (The icy Atlantic gives the body a thrilling shock – it can cure hangovers and even jet lag.) But today nothing worked till we started the marathon – both parts again – and Doctor Theatre kicked in. It's just adrenalin, I believe. Some American study claimed that when an actor goes onstage, the adrenalin is equivalent to being in a car crash. So a press performance must be like a plane crash. But this isn't useful thinking...

Sunday 13 April

I've lost more weight. My cheekbones *are* surfacing. It's a race against time.

More worrying, I think I'm getting that cough which has afflicted me in the past. I used to think it was from living next to the river, but now I wonder if it's being caused by wearing soaking-wet clothes for hours on end: throughout the show, the body suit and my vest are drenched with sweat. It can't be good for the chest. To think that the rest of the company had that terrible coughing illness which swept through the building, and are over it, and now I'm feeling this tiny, deadly tickle in the throat, just in time for the big day. Greg says I'm to just say NO to it. Trouble is, he was brought up by a down-to-earth Yorkshire mother who had no truck with illness. My mother was a Jewish hypochondriac.

The irony is – a cough like this led to that ghastly performance of *Köpenick*, which in turn led to me deciding to playing Falstaff...

Talking of which, have I captured him now, is my performance there?

The role is immensely complex. Some of it has only fallen into place during the preview period: after that first *sight* of him in my dressing-room mirror, the discussion about his *youth* with Greg, and discovering the *relationship* with a live audience. On the one hand, these growth surges have come rather late; on the other, thank God they've come at all...

I do a sketch – like the ones of other actors playing the role – but now of *my* Falstaff. I compare it with the first image I drew of him (15/11/13). There's a vital difference. Then he was sitting back – now he's heaving forward, eyes gleaming, mouth open. I'd subtitle it APPETITE (his primary characteristic, I believe): not just for food and drink, subversiveness and danger, but for *life*. [*Photo insert, page 8, My Falstaff*]

Monday 14 April

Woke with a peculiar feeling. Now that Sunday's over, there's no safe barrier left – between me and Wednesday, the press day. Maybe people who are going to have a major operation feel like this. Except I'm both patient and surgeon. With the endurance of the one, and the skill of the other. Falstaff will either come back to glorious life for the critics, or do the opposite.

Tuesday 15 April

Bad sleep. Coughing. Yet it isn't occurring during the day, or affecting the performances. It's like I'm half in control of it. Greg and his mother are half-right.

Anyway, the sun is shining, and the big sycamore outside our window is in leaf. Our view is of its inside body, the branches rippling with river light. All this spring brightness fills me with energy, aggressive energy. Fuck it, I've done all I can, I've done my best. Let tomorrow come.

Wednesday 16 April

Took one and a half sleeping pills last night – no coughing – but I still wake much too early, of course.

Before we leave the flat, we exchange first-night cards. Both express similar sentiments. His says, 'How could we nearly *not* have done this?' Mine says, 'Thank you for your craziness and bravery in giving me this part.' It's also a chance for me to comment on his production. All the things I've been admiring – Stephen's design, Tim's lighting, Paul's music, the cast's performances – they all start with Greg's vision. I've always felt these two plays have his name on them. And he's brought his three main gifts to the table: clarity, imagination, and heart. It's beautiful work.

The company, myself included, are mystified that our first call is at Trinity Church. Jasper says, 'Are we going to pray for a miracle?' But it's not God that Greg wants us to honour, but one very mortal man who happens to have been baptised and buried here. The company mood is festive – people are wearing sunglasses and T-shirts – you'd think we were going on holiday rather than embarking on our toughest marathon day yet. Greg gathers us into a circle in the churchyard, and quietly gives a rousing speech: 'We're entering a hall of mirrors. The critics are unlikely to reflect accurately what we've done. Some may flatter, some may distort. It's important for us to step into this hall of mirrors together, as a company, to know what *we* think of our work, before others start telling us what *they* think.' Then he takes us into the church, and, because of his special influence here, is able to escort us past the barrier at the Chancel, so that we can stand round Shakespeare's grave itself.

Have to confess that while the company is looking elsewhere – as Greg is doing a bit of tour-guide patter – I kneel briefly, touch the magic stone and bring my fingers to my lips.

After the church visit, everything goes into fast-forward for me: doing my make-up in the dressing room, while cards and gifts keep arriving, or people pop in to wish me well – including Ciss on her stick (I'm touched by that) – and then, before I know it, the solemn, majestic music of the opening motet, 'Urbs beata Jerusalem', is booming over the tannoy, and we're off.

First impression is that the audience is friendly. Odd. As I hurry to my next scene, I say to the actors whom I pass, 'What's the matter with them – don't they know this is a press performance?!' All is going well, but after the interval, I start to get that press–performance feeling: just getting through it, no sense of enjoyment or inspiration.

At the end, a great ovation… great cheer for me…

Greg comes to my dressing room. He says, 'You're on splendid form.' Then suddenly becomes emotional: 'When you all came on for the curtain call, I was so proud of what you'd all done.'

I hug him: 'Be proud of what *you've* done.'

I become strangely tense during the break. Manage to eat half a sandwich and a banana, but can't snooze. Go through *all* the lines of *Part II*.

Bump into Trevor in the corridor. He's had a stupendous surprise. At the end of the matinee, he was called down to the stage door, and found his parents standing there. They'd flown over from Canada. Everyone kept it a secret. I can't help picturing how two South Africans (now deceased) might have done the same thing.

Part II goes well. Though the house isn't quite full. (Couldn't the RSC have made sure it *was*?) Do I make any mistakes with the lines? Minor maybe. Can't really remember. Didn't cough. Sure of that. Then finally it's over.

They say Lear is the Everest of acting. Well, the two halves of Falstaff make for quite a mountain range too.

I need a party like a hole in the head, but have to attend. There's food – thank God – I'm starving. Manage to fill a plate, but am then surrounded by people, and can't get a morsel to my mouth.

I'm being churlish. The compliments are worth going hungry for.

David Edgar, twinkling wickedly: 'The *Henries* are my two favourite Shakespeares. So I was sure Greg and you would fuck them up. And to my astonishment, you didn't!'

Adrian Noble is generous in his praise (very generous given that he did the acclaimed production with Robert Stephens), and goes on one of his wonderful riffs about the difference of tone in the two plays: 'It's as if in the middle of a symphony, the conductor suddenly dismisses half the orchestra, and brings in new musicians who're going to do surprising things – Nigel Kennedy is now on violin and Keith Jarrett is on piano!'

Mike Poulton says: 'It's the best I've seen.'

My agent Paul Lyon-Maris says he was enthralled by the shows, and my work: 'Who'd've ever thought of you playing that part?'

'Exactly,' I say; 'It was so unlikely, I had to ask if you thought I could do it.'

Meanwhile, Greg is surrounded by the support team that have seen him through today: best friends Thelma Holt and Richard Sharples, sister Jo, and the family from Wales: Elizabeth, Will and Alice.

At last we slip away. Emerging from the stage door, we breathe deeply. The smell of Stratford. We say it as one: 'Good air!'

Friday 18 April

It's 7 p.m. The performance is about to start. From my dressing room, there's a fine view across the river: a sunny evening, the big green lawns, the long blue shadows of the willows, people strolling along the paths. It's a bank holiday – Good Friday – and Stratford is packed with visitors. It's like the whole world is at leisure, except for us in this theatre. *Part I* tonight, both parts tomorrow. But I feel peaceful, I feel good.

We've had four-star reviews across the board. The show is deemed a success, as is my performance.

Ahead, there are exciting things: the two Live-from-Stratford broadcasts, the move to our new house, and then in July a fortnight's holiday. *A holiday?* Impossible. But it's when *Two Gentlemen of Verona* opens and starts to share the repertoire. Until then, we're holding it on our own, eight times a week; until then, for me it's just Falstaff, Falstaff, Falstaff...

Now that I'm playing it, the question is: why is the role not considered one of those which the classical actor measures himself against? Shakespeare has mapped out the career of the (male) classical actor very sumptuously: in his youth, he can play Romeo, Hamlet, Richard II, Hal/Henry V; a few years later there's Macbeth, Richard III, Coriolanus, Iago, Benedick, Petruchio, Leontes, Timon; and in his mature age, Lear, Prospero, Titus, Shylock, Antony, Othello. Falstaff isn't automatically on the list. Why not? We know that Olivier turned it down – yet think of what his powers of transformation and comic inventiveness would have brought to the part. Or Gielgud – think of his wit, his melancholy dignity, the seediness he had in *No Man's Land*; he would truly have been the Don Quixote of Falstaffs. Yet of that generation of actors – probably the greatest that has been – only Richardson and Wolfit played it. What a pity. And think of Scofield (I'd have paid in blood to see him do it), think of Donald Sinden, and indeed think of Ian McKellen…! Why have these actors not tackled Falstaff? It's a mystery to me.

Over the tannoy: '*Henry IV* company, this is your beginners' call…'

I must get ready. Go downstairs to the stage. Crawl into position in the dark. Have the bedding piled on top of me. Feel the truck move down. Then I'll hear Alex do a big stretching yawn and jump off the bed. It's my cue. I'll throw back the quilts, and say:

'Now Hal, what time of day is it, lad?'

Epilogue

Tuesday 23 April

A day in the life of a show:

8.30 a.m. My cough is definitely *real*, and at its worst in the morning – awful, hacking spasms. Greg suggested I try antibiotics. Trouble is, they can cause stomach upsets. If peeing is tricky in a body suit, can you imagine diarrhoea? Anyway, there's good cause to put my woes aside. This is a great and important day: Shakespeare's birthday – his 450th! There's a firework display after tonight's performance. The organisers could probably wish for better weather. It's grey, sometimes drizzly.

10.45 a.m. Good news. Ages ago, the publisher Nick Hern got in touch, and asked if I'd like to write one of my theatre journals about playing Falstaff. I said we'd have to wait and see how the shows were received. This morning, he emailed with an unequivocal yes! I'm delighted. A new focus for my mind during the long run ahead.

12.15 p.m. Greg pops home, suddenly appearing at the French windows. 'Come outside,' he says excitedly. I shake my head, indicating my throat. 'Oh, just for a moment!' he insists. I step onto the lawn. The bells of Trinity Church are pealing away. 'They started at eleven, and will go on till three,' he says, his face alight; 'for Shakespeare!' It's called a Stedman Peal apparently, and is reserved for only the most special occasions, like royal weddings. We picture those bell-ringers we saw in November – most of them, ladies and gents of a certain age – and smile at the thought of them engaged in this Herculean task. Probably makes our matinee days seem easy.

4.45 p.m. Arriving at the stage door, I find a card from my grand-nephew and theatre-nut Josh. (He's over from South Africa with his family – Randall's daughter Heidi and her husband Ed – and saw *Part I* a couple of days ago.) In neat, carefully schooled handwriting he says: 'As I arrived at the theatre the adrenalin kicked in as I saw, on this momentous building, a sign that said RSC!' He calls the show 'phenomenal', says to me, 'I loved the way you played your charac-ter', and thanks us both for letting him see 'a Shakespeare show at the RSC!' It's very touching. If we could have this effect on all twelve-year-olds...

7.15 p.m. The show. *Part I* again. There's an unmistakable feeling of celebration in tonight's audience. To do with Shakespeare's birth-day primarily, but the warmth extending to us, and our work. (Even my cough was better – no emergency situations at all.)

10.20 p.m. As the curtain call finishes, Greg bounds onstage, and invites the audience to come outside with us for the fireworks. I race to my dressing room. Rachel takes off the wig as quickly as possible, and my dresser Rafiena helps me out of the costume and body suit, and then, leaving on most of my make-up, I jump into my civvies and go out into the night. I don't want to miss the next bit. An ex-traordinary sight greets me: hundreds of people standing behind barriers, gazing up at the theatre expectantly. It's like the end of *Close Encounters*. Something miraculous is about to happen. And indeed, as a little divine sign, the drizzle that had fallen all day is no more; the heavens are clear. I find Greg in one of the control tents. There are squads of health and safety people, security people, fire officers. Greg goes onto a podium on the lawn, and, speaking into a mic, asks the crowd to bellow, 'Happy Birthday, Shakespeare!' The RSC band strikes up with alarum calls – trumpets and drums – familiar from a thousand productions here, and then someone, somewhere, starts pressing buttons. The first fireworks are disappointing, half out of view, behind the building. I bite my lip: *oh no, don't let this be feeble*. But then bigger and better explosions of colour begin to light up the sky above the roof – in high-leaping sprays of gold, silver, blue and red – and in front of the theatre a huge wrought-iron portrait of Shakespeare slowly takes shape in flames, a fire drawing, while be-hind it an arc of tumbling white sparks gushes down the building like a waterfall. Meanwhile the RSC band has been supplanted by a soundtrack of music: now Prokofiev's *Romeo and Juliet*, now Cole Porter's *Brush Up Your Shakespeare*, now Walton's score from Olivier's *Henry V* film. I turn to Greg. We're both grinning, both in tears. The feeling is of wonder, total wonder. Fireworks find the child in us all. Music stirs the adult. Together, the mixture is intoxicating. The crowd cheers again and again. Shakespeare's giant face is fully alight now – how pagan, we're burning our god! – yet his expression remains as still and unreadable as ever. Though I like to think that in the church down the road, his bones are tapping along to the tunes.

11 p.m. Walking home to Avonside, I feel dazed. How wonderful to be here, in this town, on this particular night. I have just played one of Drama's classic roles in a production which Greg directed, in the theatre that he runs, and then we joined all those people to pay homage to the playwright who made it all possible, the local boy made good. It's one of those moments when I realise I've been sleep-walking through my job, and then suddenly wake up, and see it for what it truly is, and it's completely bloody amazing. Sartre said that there's a God-shaped hole in all of us. Greg fills his with Shakespeare; the other day he said, laughing, 'I'm not the director of a company, I'm the priest of a religion!' And me? I have Falstaff inside me now – I can say it confidently at last – and that great, greedy, glorious bastard leaves no room for anything else at all.

www.nickhernbooks.co.uk

facebook.com/nickhernbooks

twitter.com/nickhernbooks